Ghost Quest

New Hampshire's
Paranormal Research Society

Beckah Tolley, Raven Duclos, and Katie Boyd

Schiffer Publishing Ltd

4880 Lower Valley Road, Atglen, Pennsylvania 19310

Published by Schiffer Publishing Ltd.
4880 Lower Valley Road
Atglen, PA 19310
Phone: (610) 593-1777; Fax: (610) 593-2002
E-mail: Info@schifferbooks.com

For the largest selection of fine reference books on this and related subjects, please visit our web site at **www.schifferbooks.com.** We are always
looking for people to write books on new and related subjects. If you
have an idea for a book please contact us at the above address.

This book may be purchased from the publisher.
Include $3.95 for shipping.
Please try your bookstore first.
You may write for a free catalog.

In Europe, Schiffer books are distributed by
Bushwood Books
6 Marksbury Ave.
Kew Gardens
Surrey TW9 4JF England
Phone: 44 (0) 20 8392-8585; Fax: 44 (0) 20 8392-9876
E-mail: info@bushwoodbooks.co.uk
Website: www.bushwoodbooks.co.uk
Free postage in the U.K., Europe; air mail at cost.

Designed by "Sue"
Type set in A Charming Font Expanded/NewBskvll BT
Ouija® is a registered trademark of Parker Brother's Games
ISBN: 978-0-7643-2886-2
Printed in China

Schiffer Books are available at special discounts for bulk purchases for
sales promotions or premiums. Special editions, including personalized
covers, corporate imprints, and excerpts can be created in large quanti-
ties for special needs. For more information contact the publisher.

Disclaimer

Within this book are true accounts of haunting, paranormal activity, our experiences, and evidence. Some names, both crew and client have been changed to protect the identity and privacy of each person. Ghost Quest is an experienced, highly trained paranormal research group. Inexperienced groups, or people trying this out for themselves, please do your research, or better yet get a professional researcher to come with you on hunts. Remember, you never know what you're going into, and what may seem very quiet, may indeed harbor something more darker.

Notes:

❖   We do not advocate going to private property for hunts. Remember to ALWAYS get permission before entering any property, even for cemeteries.

❖   Only experienced mediums should attempt to contact spirits. If you are not a trained medium, have one with you; if you can't, don't do it!

❖   Although Ghost Quest does go into cemeteries, we do so with respect and honor. We do not advocate the destruction of any property located within the boundaries of cemetery walls. We will report anyone we find destroying such property to the authorities.

Acknowledgements

We would like to thank Dinah Roseberry from Schiffer Publishing for making this book possible, Thomas D'Agostino and Renee Mallett for mentioning us in their books *Haunted New Hampshire* and *Manchester Ghosts* respectively. Thanks to all those wonderful people who allowed us into their homes and businesses and let us have our run of them. A special thanks to Mr. Ludwig of Manchester Parks and Recreations for letting us into Valley Street. A very special thanks to the Ghost Quest crew members who have come and gone. Even though you are not here with us, we wish you the very best with your own Ghost Questing.

A thanks to the friends of Valley Street for all your hard work! It's paying off. A final thanks to Rayna for your jokes and all the coffee …. you kept us laughing and kept us going!! You're the best!

Dedication

This book is dedicated to Doug Warren and Fred Turner our long lost Ghost Quest brothers—never give up the Quest.

Contents

About The Authors

Raven Duclos

Raven has long been in touch with her psychic gifts. She has been reading for people from the age of thirteen and seeing and talking to spirits since she was four. Throughout her life she has amazed people and herself with her abilities. She often didn't believe she saw what she was seeing, but after validation from some very important people in her life, she took her abilities a bit more seriously. She began to seek. During her period of seeking (which in truth has never stopped), she gained spiritual truths and insights by researching many paths and traditions. Her experimentation only served to open her mind to the varied types of phenomena out there and her other abilities. Raven continues to have a strong spiritual and mystical orientation, and her intuition is multi-faceted and complex.

Beckah Tolley

Beckah grew up in a family of psychically gifted people and she was encouraged to use her own abilities to help others. At fourteen she was giving readings in her school cafeteria for change so she could get soft drinks at the end of the day. By eighteen she had taken up the family business, contacting spirits and giving psychic con-

sultations. Now, at twenty-two, she has expanded upon her abilities and divination techniques, being able to use both modern and ancient divination systems and widening her psychic field. This includes: reading energy, auras, spirits, past lives, pets, and more. Beckah is happily married, with four cats (her babies) and lives in New Hampshire.

Katie Boyd

As a young girl, Katie had been fascinated with the strange and unexplained. This lead Katie to years of deep integrated studies and hands-on work both with teachers and on her own. This culminated in Katie earning two degrees in Occult sciences. Now older and wiser, Katie has over fifteen

years of demonology and occult science under her belt. She specializes in magical seals, symbols, demonic issues, possessions, and occult crimes. Katie is married and resides in New Hampshire.

Crew List

Raven

Her job: Raven is a Lead Investigator/Psychic Medium/Web Mistress.

Background: Raven is one of the four founding members of Ghost Quest. She has had extensive experience both in her practice as a psychic medium and in her ghost research dealing with all types of spiritual energy.

Beckah

Her job: Beckah is an Investigator/Medium/Energy Reader.

Background: Beckah, along with Raven and Katie, is one of the founders of Ghost Quest. She has a long history of dealing with the paranormal and seeing energy that is vital when looking for entities or portals.

Katie

Her job: Katie is an Investigator/Demonologist/Occult Sciences Expert.

Background: Katie is also a founding member and has extensive knowledge of demonology, exorcisms, and ceremonial magic, including symbology and sigil making. This is critically important when we're dealing with more than a mere haunting.

Doug

His job: Investigator.

Background: Doug is an expert on astral planes and their connection to our consciousness, and is sensitive to both spirits and portals.

Fred

His job: Investigator/Sensitive/Coffee Cake Man.

Background: Fred has a past deeply rooted in the paranormal together with his own experiences, and what he experienced under Doug's tutelage gave him a wide spectrum of knowledge on which to base his findings. (And we kept him around for the coffee cake!)

Ghost Quest The First Years

Ghost Quest is the brain child of Raven Duclos, Beckah Tolley, Katie Boyd, Doug Warren, and Fred Turner. From the moment Raven and Beckah did their first ghost hunt with a friend, they were hooked. It wasn't long before the others joined them. After five or six such investigations they realized they had formed a group and decided to put a name to it. Ghost Quest.

Ghost Quest was, from the beginning, a group filled with true characters. They had Raven, who touted herself as a "Large Medium;" Beckah, with her nose ring and her pink baseball cap forever perched on her head; Katie, with her consistent cup of coffee in hand; Doug, always looking for portals; and Fred with his awesome coffee cake.

It took a while for them to grow as friends and colleagues. There were many discrepancies, arguments, tears, and much laughter.

Raven, at the time, owned a small metaphysical store in Manchester. Beckah worked with her, and together, they did readings and had gatherings at the store. It was during one of these gatherings that they first met Doug Warren. He was an interesting fellow and a master at astral travel. A sensitive, Doug could spot a portal at a mile away. He came to the shop looking to teach trance dance, and although that didn't take off, our friendship did. Soon we invited him to go ghost hunting with us, and boy was he up for the task! He loved taking his camera and getting pictures, or listening to the EVPs we had just gotten. He was exciting to be around; you literally could feed off his energy.

The next person to come in was Katie Boyd. Katie was also someone who had come to our gatherings. As soon as she had heard about our ghost hunting exploits, she told us about her background. Demonology. Well if you're going to study something, might as well make it big! At least we knew with

Katie along we would be more than protected, as her abilities to control and seal dark forces were incredible! Katie is still with Ghost Quest to this day as one of our founding members and still performing her role as demonologist. Katie you go girl!

Next to come on board was Fred Turner. What can we say about Fred? He is such a character! He is an absolute doll with coffee cake! Seriously, he is a sensitive and an empath, who was ever seeking to expand his knowledge, and as valuable as that was to the team, it was his quick wit and good-natured sarcasm that won everyone over. There were many serious and intense investigations that Fred's wry humor really relaxed everyone.

So, together, this motley crew began to investigate places. Starting small, they went to local cemeteries. The beginning investigations were filled with firsts for all the members. At one cemetery in particular, Doug and Katie saw their first imps. These are dark little creatures about three and a half feet tall that move very fast. Doug freaked out a bit, staring in wonder and then looking at us with eyes wide and a huge grin on his face—pure amazement at what he had seen, while Katie was doubting her own eyesight until she realized others saw them, too. Then a loud "Wahoo!!" could be heard as she realized she saw something phenomenal. Raven was getting yelled at and freaking out completely as she realized no one else had heard a thing. Beckah became possessed by the spirit of a young woman and Fred felt heart attacks when he was, in fact, fine. These were just some of the things we encountered during our cases. We each knew what had to be done and we did it. It wasn't always clock work, but a lot of it was.

As fun as the investigations were, we had a blast in between them. We took time to hang out together and really got to know each other. We spent time honing our skills, both psychic and technical. Each took turns giving classes in their particular area or just played around building our psychic repertoire. These were fun and often bonding moments for the crew. This was when we let it all hang out, our past, our issues, and we supported each other much like true brothers and sisters. Because of this, our ghost hunting was one hundred percent better than it would have been if it was just a job. There was true love there, and respect for each other and our chosen fields.

So thus began the first team and it was not soon after that we began to document our cases…

It Started With a Church

Devil's Church

Raven and Beckah, both psychic consultants, have learned to accept the paranormal, spirits, and energy as a part of their daily living. As such they met other people with similar interests. On one such occasion, a friend came over for dinner and began to talk about a legend surrounding an abandoned church in Manchester with many eyewitness and second-hand stories of satanic practice. As they had never thought of seeking out spirits (the spirits usually found *them*) the three friends' curiosity was peaked and they began to research the area.

Paranormal phenomenon runs rampant within the stories that the Ghost Quest crew have heard floating around, specifically two light-skinned monks with glowing red eyes are said to be seen every Halloween on the property. Raven and Beckah were greatly intrigued by the stories they had heard from friends, and decided on a whim to go and investigate this mysterious building. They passed the dilapidated building once before finding it; the church itself was covered in graffiti depicting devils and upside down pentagrams, there were no glass in the windows, no doors, and it was thoroughly trashed. Dragonflies surrounded the building, which to Raven meant protection, she immediately knew this was going to be fun!

When they first entered the building there was a suffocating heaviness, and an unwelcoming feeling. Raven immediately began to sense a female energy within the building and the multitude of deaths that local lore tells us went on there. Beckah was drawn to an area in the back of the church where they later found out the altar would have been located, and began to see flashes of men dressed in dark robes around the 1950s—but she felt that what she was seeing went back

The sign above the door in Greek means, " Prophets of the Sun."

further than that. Beckah, who channels spirits, commenced a session. Following is the information we gathered.

A man named Edgar immigrated to this area; his own father ran the church in a small English community. He was a trans-generational satanic practitioner and founded the Church in Manchester in the late 1940s-early 1950s. It was located on his property; he was grooming his son to follow in his footsteps. He wasn't a powerful man but was respected within his community of land owners, having had a two- to three-story house on the property, as well as a stables or a carriage house. There were at least twenty other worshippers with him and many sacrifices made, mostly animal, but a couple of women as well. We felt they were sacrificed due to fear of the women escaping.

During Beckah's session, she led the group outside to a drywell, making motions of throwing a body in. Raven later experienced a vision of a woman with shoulder-length brown hair crawling out of the well. Although we did not get a picture of this woman, before leaving Raven decided to take a couple extra shots of the abandoned building's back window and

Lady ghost shoulder as she leaves frame of photo.

got the shock of her life when a full-bodied crystal-clear apparition appeared in her LED screen. She immediately took another shot and got the picture of the woman's shoulder. The lady ghost did not seem to acknowledge our presence.

We immediately deemed the building haunted, and though it was a wild ride for our first time, we were happy to leave and thought the episode over.

WE WERE WRONG!!!

When we returned to our headquarters (Raven's house at this time), we immediately went to check out our cool finds. We had one tape recorder going during the investigation, and although we didn't get any impressive EVPs, we were excited over the photographs. As we went through the evidence, we discovered there was more to the white woman picture than we had thought. We'd also caught the brown-haired woman in the corner looking very out of focus and creepy. Additionally, there were two other pictures of faces coming out of the wall. Although these pictures were also impressive, we were still reeling from the lady ghost picture.

We saved them on the computer, which later presented its own problems when Raven found several of her business disks mysteriously ending up with the same photos from the church on them.

It was when we were going over the history of the building that the phenomena began. The first thing we looked for was what the sign above the church meant. We soon found out the Greek letters formed the title "Prophets of the Sun"—that is as far as we got; the computer was turned off from the back switch. Raven and Beckah looked at each other for a moment and in stereo said, "OOOOKKKAAAYYY."

We turned on the computer and continued our research undeterred by the event, until we heard scraping across the floor. We looked down and what we saw was enough to almost make us wet our pants—the blonde lady had decided to follow us home. She dragged herself, arm over arm, across the floor, entirely naked. We knew that the only way to help her was to find out what happened.

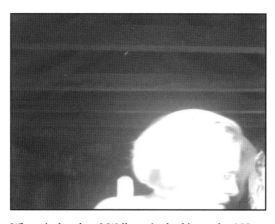

Where is the ghost? Well, you're looking at her! Here is a picture of the woman who followed us home.

So we continued to search, and we found through the name of the church that it was indeed a satanic sect that worshipped a high demonic entity. Slayings of animals and people both were promoted within this sect to feed the greed of the demon and followers. There were also many other unsavory bits about this organization. But that is as far as we got, because the computer turned off, forever.

What is a ghost hunter to do? We decided, under the circumstances, we had gotten enough information and proceeded with a clearing in our home to remove the blonde woman. We successfully connected her with other helpful spirits that accompanied her to the spirit realm.

Six months later, we developed the courage to return yet again in an official ghost quest with a team of five members, including Beckah, Raven, Fred Turner, Doug Warren, Sandy K., and Ben K. This time, we went in there armed with tape recorders, cameras, and lots of bravado. We thought our previous experiences had taught us the *do's and don'ts*.

Ghost Quest brings you this Public Service Announcement! WE WERE WRONG AGAIN!!

We all walked in and Beckah was drawn yet again to the altar, found a broom (Lord knows where), and proceeded to sweep off the altar floor space. When Raven and crew asked why she was doing this, she replied, "I feel I need to make this clean. I can't stop." Raven then insisted Beckah be removed from the church and Beckah adamantly refused. Doug and Ben had to then escort her out of the church and into the clearing behind it.

Those who remained within the walls began to experience the same phenomena, a sensation of being punched on the left cheek. When Raven tried to discover why the spirits were creating this impression on the crew members, she discovered it was due to the dark-haired woman that we had run into in the previous investigation.

Sandy and Beckah discovered a trail leading into the woods behind the church. There they discovered several stone benches and a fire pit. The smell surrounding the area was of burning hair and flesh. Beckah and Sandy immediately turned around and headed back to the church, not being able to handle the smell or the residual energy surrounding the area.

When they arrived back at the building, only two members remained inside, Beckah went into the church again with Raven, while Doug and Sandy took a more extensive look at the property, finding what looked like old unmarked graves. Raven took pictures of Doug and Sandy as they returned up the path and was amazed to find yet another full-body apparition grace her LED screen. This time the brown-haired woman was the primary spirit.

Upon completion of this investigation, we went back to GQHQ (Ghost Quest Headquarters—now Raven's Metaphysical Store) where Raven noticed Beckah was acting a little bit *off*. The more Raven questioned Beckah, the more strange she got, and the more Raven knew this was not her colleague.

At this point, a clearing had begun on Beckah. She became agitated, angry, swearing, spitting, and this culminated in trying to burn a colleague with a cigarette. After twenty minutes of attempting to clear Beckah, it seemed successful; her normal composure was once again apparent.

After the clearing, Ben felt a presence on his back; Beckah picked up a fantasy-styled double-headed axe and said, "I can clear him." Raven recognized that the spirit was still in control of Beckah, but not before she swung the axe one quarter inch from Ben's back. Raven relinquished the axe from Beckah and continued the clearing again. This time the female spirit was connected with her grandmother and taken to the other side.

Not soon after Katie joined us and learned of our experiences at the church, she decided to venture up and see if she could verify or disprove the information the psychics related to her. While alone up at the church, she saw an inhuman animal, almost fox like, circling the outside of the church at an extremely fast pace. She knew this was definitely the site of negative occult magic as an inhuman animal such as the one we just described was often set up to protect the ritual site.

A Devil's Church Story submitted by a guest of our website

"I have a really good story about Devil's Church in Manchester, New Hampshire. Probably about ten years ago, we were bored and looking for something to do. We decided to go and check out the church and see if it was really haunted. We had a friend drive us there and when we got out of the car we decided to leave the headlights on to be able to see inside the building, because we didn't have flashlights. We also left the car running as not to drain the battery. We were joking around and poking fun at the stories behind the building and proceeded to go inside.

Upon entering the building, I walked up to where the supposed alter is, stood on it and said "F--- you Satan," and spit on the floor. As soon as my spit hit the floor, the car stalled and the headlights went out. As if that is not weird enough, here comes the really strange part. The other people who we were with me had their car and said that they would just start their car up and give us a jump—their car wouldn't start either.

We all split up and went to try to find someone to help us start the cars (or at least find a pay phone to use because, yes this was before everyone in the world had a cell phone). My friend and I, who were the only two who had made fun upon entering the building, went off together and everybody else paired up and went off together. Now at this time we were both fifteen and it was 2:30 in the morning so we happened to get picked up by the police for being out after curfew.

Once we talked to our friends with the vehicles after this whole ordeal, we found that apparently the vehicles started up again without any help at all, pretty much at the same time that we got picked up by the police. Could've just been a coincidence, but an awful creepy one if that is the case. It really did seem as if there was a presence of some sort; who knows, I could just be being paranoid. What do you think? Strange huh?"

Evidence

Evidence came in many forms at Devil's Church. Photo's, EVPs, and personal experiences abound. Below is a listing of evidence that we obtained from this case.

A spirit stands behind one of our crew members.

Photos:
    Lady Ghost
    Lady Ghost's shoulder
    Orbs With Doug
    Dark Woman With Sandy, Ben and Doug (3 pictures)
    Blue Face of a Male in The Wall
    White Face Going "oooooh"

EVPs:
    "Hi"
    Heart Beats (on two tape recorders)
    Crying

Personal Experiences:
    Sandy was touched on the arm
    All members felt they had been hit on the back of the neck with a spike
    Beckah felt highly emotional and also later very drained
    Raven felt pin pricks
    Doug was light headed

The altar as it originally stood on Beckah and Raven's first trip to Devil's Church.

Historical Facts About Baal and His Followers

We tracked Prophets of the Sun to the God Baal, here are some of the things we learned about this ancient entity.

* ❖ He was worshipped around the time of Canaanites and the Phoenicians.
* ❖ His name translates to "Lord," "Master," and even "Husband."
* ❖ Kings and royalty of the ten biblical tribes worshipped Baal.
* ❖ He was an accepted god among the ancient Jewish culture and was worshipped among the masses who depended on him as God of the Sun, for prosperity and productivity of their crops and livestock.
* ❖ Within the religion, there was a hierarchy of priests and devotees; many separate sects were established in his name.
* ❖ The ceremonies mainly focused on the element of fire as it was attributed to the sun; they burnt incense, offered sacrifices (sometimes human) which were also burned.
* ❖ The priests danced around altars, chanted, and cut themselves with knives hoping to get the god's attention and compassion.
* ❖ Some of the priests had sacred prostitutes who helped perform sexual rituals to promote fertility.
* ❖ They cut no corners if you did something wrong; punishments varied from being beaten to being killed.

After researching the cult, we came to the conclusion that what our mediums tapped into was a sect trying to recreate the old practices of the Prophets of the Sun.

Though this case may seem like a frighteningly good time, we caution you to neither attempt channeling, clearing, or contacting spirits without training, or a trained professional with you. The axe used by Beckah in this case was a blunt edged sacred tool that she primarily uses during clearings, hence why it didn't seem obvious when Beckah exclaimed she could clear him. But even professionals can get taken over; no one is immune. Please take caution before attempting any investigations or spirit contact.

Do not attempt to go to the Devil's Church; they tore it down over a year and a half ago, but for an unknown reason, nothing has been built and there is only a giant crater where the church used to be.

Crew Afterthoughts

Raven: Devil's Church was our first, and for me one of our scariest investigations. This isn't based on the investigation itself, although seeing all the dragonflies and everyone getting such a severe headache in the same place did raise some huge goose bumps for me. It was the after effects. The spirit following us home, crashing the computer, possessing Beckah. It was hair raising and I wouldn't step foot back in that area again. Although older and wiser now, I shudder to think what might follow us back.

Beckah: This place will always be stuck in my memory, although the second time around I don't remember much! I think the Church was a fascinating paranormal find and I look back now wishing to hell we had recorded the activity that went on at the house! It was my first leap into investigations and a great christening!

Katie: I feel it was a highly negative and demonic site, and I wish it was still standing because it is a demonologist's dream! Are you sure I can't take a piece of it home?

Devil's Church as it stands today—a great gaping hole in the earth.

Valley Street Cemetery

"Don't leave me whatever you do!"
—EVP from Valley Street Cemetery

A constant hangout throughout the years of Ghost Quest, Valley Street Cemetery is near and dear to the GQ Crew's heart. The group first heard about Valley from a crew member who had claimed she experienced phenomena near their famous Smyth mausoleum. It is located on a very heavily trafficked street, but the cemetery itself is oddly silent, almost sound-proof!

Valley Street Cemetery is a sprawling expanse of beauti-fully tended gravesites. As you walk through, the first thing you notice is an ornate brick chapel complete with spires and the infamous Smyth mausoleum which sit almost side by side. The main cemetery branches off in two directions. On one side, you are led to another smaller mausoleum; on the other, you follow the path that is littered with graves on either side. This path takes you down into a gorgeous field of flora and fauna with a mowed lawn centering the area. From here you are about twenty to thirty feet lower than where the chapel sits. During the day, this cemetery is welcoming and serene; but at night, it changes drastically.

The first time the crew went there, it was daytime and the activity was low. They did notice the headstones around the Smyth were knocked over or broken in half; they at-tributed this to vandals having a laugh at the cemeteries. This saddened the whole crew. They didn't experience any phenomena and were so disappointed. Not being daunted by this, Doug suggested they go back once more during the day "just to make sure." There was a bit of dissention among the group, some of who expressed that the group shouldn't go back when there was no evidence of phenomena happening.

The back of the Smyth Mausoleum where a prostitute fell to her death.

After about an hour of talking, they all agreed and decided to wait a week or two before revisiting this beautiful site.

On a bright and sunny fall afternoon, Doug, Raven, Fred, Beckah, and Katie piled into the car and took off towards Valley Street. Most of the crew were secretly hoping not to be disappointed again, but outwardly seemed optimistic. With tools in hand and smiling faces, they began their investigation. This time the crew was not let down!

They went around the cemetery to get a feel for the energies that dwelled within, but no matter where they were, they ended up at the Smyth mausoleum. This mausoleum is huge and simplistic in design. It is also set backwards facing away from the road, almost as if the owners wanted the residents to have a beautiful view of the setting sun and the lawn which rested so far below.

There is a legend to this crypt that the crew had heard about. It seems that in the late sixties a young woman, who was a prostitute, fell to her death after conducting business near the front door of the Smyth. Rumors abound of people seeing her or hearing evidence of her. The exact circumstances of her death are unknown by Ghost Quest, as for the rumor…read on.

Raven and Fred carefully walked around the outer edge of the structure until they arrived at the front. Raven looked down over the edge and quickly stepped back. Fred was amazed at the drop and stated that he was shocked that someone would have constructed this in so dangerous a way. The first thing they noticed was the graffiti that was strewn all over the façade. Upset that anyone would sink to this level, they began taking pictures, hoping to put them on the website and help curb future instances of this.

Fred thought he heard something scraping inside the mausoleum. He said that it sounded like someone dragging something heavy and metal. They began to take flash photos inside the peepholes of the doorway. After about twenty shots, they left and walked back toward the chapel.

Unbeknownst to Raven and Fred, Beckah and Katie were approaching the Smyth from the other side, and began taking photos of the cliff drop and into the peep holes. Raven, who was now approaching the path, suddenly heard loud in her right ear, "GET THE F--- AWAY FROM THE DOOR!" Raven's heart began to beat at a frantic pace as she was trying to process what just happened. She screamed at Fred "Did you hear that?!?"

Fred meekly asked, "Hear what?"

Raven then saw Katie and Beckah emerge from behind Smyth. She screamed, "What did you yell?!? Did you yell something?!?"

Both Katie and Beckah shook their heads no and Beckah asked what happened. Raven kept repeating, "I am so out of here!!" over and over. Unknown to the crew, this is one of the first times Raven had heard spirit outside of her head. She was totally freaked out, not so much from the hearing of it, as the fact that no one else had heard it.

The crew members gathered as they thought this had been enough for one day. The drive home was conducted

The chapel at Valley Street; local lore tells us that someone committed suicide here.

in silence and they also realized that first impressions were not always true.

Back at the headquarters, while going over gathered evidence and having coffee and cake, Katie set up the tape recorders. After a half hour of listening Raven's face brightened measurably and a smile graced her face. There on the tape were the words, as if from a distance… "Away from the door!" She knew she had not lost her sanity and all was right with the world. There were other EVPs, but none as remarkable as the silent scream that echoed in one woman's ear.

It took Raven a while before she was willing to go back to Valley Street, and luckily the crew was very understanding about this.

A couple weeks later they decided it was time to go back. Katie, Beckah, Raven, and a guest got in the car and made their way over to Valley. Again it was daytime, and as the four got out of the car, Raven heard, "Don't come over here!"

This was not a shout, but a firm request. Raven opted to stay behind as the others bravely went on to face whatever was inside the Smyth mausoleum. As they rounded the corner, they listened intently for any sound or movement. There was nothing to be heard. As soon as they stood in front of the door, a heaviness settled on them and they felt as if they were being watched. They looked at each other, shrugged and took out their camera and tape recorder.

Suddenly, they saw movement and looked up. There in the corner of the doorway, through a high peephole, came a wasp. This was followed by two, then three, then a dozen. They walked calmly, but very quickly back to the car. Katie, out of breath said, "When that woman wants to make a point, she makes a point!"

After catching their breath, the crew began to explore other parts of the cemetery. Beckah spotted a shadow man walking through and drew everyone's attention to him. He looked solid enough, but was very dark, and he walked at a leisurely pace from one side to the other before disappearing. It wasn't till later that confirmation of what they had seen came through.

It seems that this spirit is also centered at the Smyth. No one knows who he is, but he has been heard and seen by those who visit Valley Street, and sightings of him have been said to precede destruction of headstones there. It made us wonder if he was the real reason the female ghost didn't want people over by the door. Was she protecting us or him?

This is where our psychics picked up mass burials due to sickness. Later, this was confirmed.

Evidence

The evidence at Valley Street Cemetery was overwhelming. There were extensive photos, EVPs and personal experiences. Below is a listing of evidence from this case.

Photos:
Flora's Headstone Orb
Smyth Mausoleum Orb
Chapel Orbs
Small Mausoleum Energies
Peek-a-boo Face
Garden Orbs

EVPS:
"Away From The Door"
Heavy breathing
"Don't Leave Me" (Female)
"Don't Leave Me Whatever You Do" (Male)
Growl
"Raven"

Flora's grave, a favorite spirit of Ghost Quest.

Personal Experiences:
Unfortunately, there were no other experiences than those already related in the story.

Historical Facts of Valley Street Cemetery
❖ Valley Street was built on twenty acres in 1840 as a garden cemetery by the Amoskeag Manufacturing Company and donated to the city of Manchester.
❖ The famous John Stark who spoke the words, "Live free or die," which later became the motto of New Hampshire, is buried within Valley's gothic gates along with thirteen private mausoleums and a host of Manchester's past mayors.
❖ In the 1850s, an outbreak of cholera caused the deaths of hundreds, and it was decided to bury their dead in the most economical way possible. Mass grave burials were performed only at night; you can recognize this site as there few headstones, they placed them across from the paupers graves on the northeast side.
❖ A young woman either committed suicide there or was murdered by the front of the Smith mausoleum, falling to her death over the edge of the cliff.

Recently, there has been a host of problems regarding headstone tipping and graffiti at the cemetery, and a wonderful organization called Friends of the Valley Cemetery have dedicated themselves to putting up new fencing and restoring the cemetery to its former glory. If you would like to donate to them or have a historical tour, their address is in the back of the book.

Crew Afterthoughts

Raven: Valley Street will always be near and dear to my heart. It wasn't one of out most extreme cases, but we always get some kind of evidence there. The reason it is so dear to me is that it was the first time on an investigation I heard someone yell at me outside my head. That, along with finding out the history of the young woman and hearing her since then, has made Valley Street so special.

Beckah: After the Church this was a nice change, active but not scary. My favorite spirit, Flora, lies in Valley Street Cemetery and she has an awesome peaceful presence. I love going there just to visit with her.

Katie: I've always been into history and this place has a lot; every time we go there, we find a new part of Valley Street and the people buried there. Seeing the headstones is like stepping back in time, and that is a joy for me.

Clara's House

"Reunited and it feels so good."
—Peaches and Herb

Ghost quest was called to investigate Clara's house; she was experiencing the feeling of being watched, toys moving of their own volition, her children would talk to people who were not there, and just a general feeling of unease within the home.

The crew, along with three guests, went to investigate this troubled family's home. Upon arriving we spoke to the woman and conducted a walkthrough. Raven and one of the crewmembers walked the house room by room sensing and conversing with the spirits that resided within the home.

During the walkthrough, Raven was called back to the group because one of the guests (Amanda) became overwhelmed with emotion and began sobbing erratically. There was no cause apparent for this emotional out burst, and even Amanda didn't know why she felt the way she did. Raven explained to her that when entering a paranormal charged home, you can become more psychically open and sensitive to the spirits around you. Spirits usually attach to a person that they feel can relate to their predicament or the spirit feels some form of connection with the affected person.

In this case, Amanda reminded the male spirit of his wife in both look and action. Raven, sensing the presence attached to Amanda, took her to a back bedroom of the house where she contacted the spirit and tried to get Amanda to sense or see the spirit herself. Information was given to Raven from the spirit indicating that he had been blamed for his child's death and remained grounded until he could tell his story of blame, anger, and innocence.

Here is the story as it was told to Raven:

He was a farmer, and where Clara's house stood was formally his farmhouse, which was no more than three rooms. His young son was three years of age. The father had left the son alone to go out to the barn. We are not sure how long the son was in the home alone, but when the father returned, the son appeared to have gone from a healthy young boy to a sickly child, vomiting, pale, and wan. Within approximately one hour, the son had passed from a form of poisoning. Everyone blamed the father for his death, assuming the father had poisoned his only son. The father continued to blame himself for his negligence even in the afterlife.

Due to the father's guilt, he had created his own hell. Raven connected this poor soul with the child he believed he killed. The reuniting was both extraordinary and emotional for both the spirits and Raven and Amanda, as they looked on in wonderment at the redemption this man had found and the joy at the peace that no longer eluded him. The psychics watched as the father carried his beautiful son back to the other side, a smile on his face as he realized he was forgiven.

A week later Ghost Quest conducted a follow up interview with the family; no phenomena has occurred since the reuniting of the father and the son.

Evidence

Unfortunately due to a technical error we lost the photos we had taken.

Photos:
Unknown

EVPs:
"Help"
"Raven"
mumbling

Personal Experiences:
Amanda felt extreme distress throughout the case.

Crew Afterthoughts

Raven: This was a great experience as it was so emotionally moving. Reuniting the male spirit with his son was a moment I will never forget. It just goes to show how wonderfully healing this work can be.

Beckah: Unfortunately, I missed the reuniting, however the energy in the place was very exciting, and the spirits I did pick up on were very welcoming. I feel that this was a wonderful investigation and that it was great to know that we really helped not only the living family, but the spirit and his family as well.

Katie: I just love a happy ending.

A House In Concord

"I still feel something!"

—Beckah

The Ghost Quest crew received an e-mail from a distraught woman in Concord. Raven called her and she related the types of phenomena she and her son had been experiencing. After a brief discussion we decided we needed to help this poor woman. Katie, Beckah, and Raven got in the car and headed off to Concord.

As we drove up, we saw a community of two-floor apartments. The area was sparse and almost looked desolate.

At first we couldn't find the house; there was no number on it. Someone just at that moment happened to walk by and the investigators asked if they knew of the house. The man looked at us as if we had two heads and pointed it out. Not understanding why the man would give us such a look, we turned our heads to where he was pointing. It was right in front of us with the number on it. We looked at each other and laughed nervously. Beckah, always one to voice what she thinks said, "Well yeah, that was weird."

Upon entering the unit, we were given a tour. The apartment consisted of two bedrooms upstairs, a kitchen, parlor, and dining space downstairs, all sparsely decorated. Neither Raven nor Beckah felt too much at this time. We went upstairs to the son's room and were immediately drawn to the closet.

"My son hates sleeping up here. He hears bangs and the closet door being moved. He feels someone touching him and he has terrible nightmares. He also feels his bed shake and thinks we are having an earthquake. He's very scared of being here and I don't know what to do!"

Beckah and Raven tried to reassure the woman that we would take care of it. But she was truly frazzled by all she had been through. She also talked about what she herself had experienced—being touched and hearing a man's voice was just a bit of the phenomena.

As we began to investigate, we were drawn into the child's bedroom. Immediately, Beckah and Raven were pulled to the closet where a dollhouse was hidden. According to his mom, the child had seen people in the dollhouse. (This was related after the clearing.)

The first occurrence of phenomena was when Katie experienced someone breathing by her ear. She jumped and related what she had heard. Raven immediately began to feel overwhelmingly hot. She was sweating and fanning with her hand, and Beckah began to feel sick to her stomach. The heat began to fade from Raven, Katie had calmed down, and the investigation continued. Raven asked Katie to take the woman downstairs so that she and Beckah could clear the upstairs areas.

When we began, Raven got in touch with three negative spirits. Not willing to leave of their own accord, Raven, with the assistance of other spirits, helped them to vacate the premises. But then Beckah said, "It's not clear."

"What are you talking about? They're gone??" Raven asked.

"I still feel something!" Beckah said as she sat on the bed. She had come to understand that because of past experiences, she should accept her abilities. The spirit would not let up. It was spreading negativity.

"Well, you need to tap into it then Beckah, because I'm not feeling it!" Raven stated.

"I'm not doing it!" stated Beckah, getting agitated with the situation.

"Look Beckah, you are a medium, this is what you do. If you're feeling something then you need to say who and what it is so we can clear it!" Raven said. At this time she was becoming concerned.

"Okay, okay, hold on," Beckah said then closed her eyes tapping in. We soon discovered that a male spirit was the source of her stomach sickness. This man was not a disturbing presence, and although the symptoms of his death pained the medium, she did not feel negativity with him. In fact, the man seemed to be protective of the home.

It turned out that his name was Jonathan and that he was the tenant's grandfather, attempting to help the family survive the negative spirits that infested the house.

With Beckah and Raven occupied upstairs, downstairs, Katie and the client were taking pictures and collecting EVPs. Katie took several pictures of a portrait of Jesus that adorned the wall. Ghostly faces manifested within the snapshots emanating from the picture. Katie was startled to see the faces on her camera but said nothing to the woman. She didn't want to scare her at this point. When the two psychics arrived back downstairs, the crew deemed the rest of the spirits helpful and not harmful in any way. The client was amazed to hear that her grandfather resided within the home, and his name and his way of passing was confirmed by the woman.

We talked with the woman for a few moments before getting ready to leave. The woman seemed to be at ease and the house felt more peaceful. Beckah, Katie, and Raven got in the car and headed to the HQ.

While the shots taken of the portrait of Jesus were great, the EVPs taken at the home were most impressive. In one instance, while getting in touch with the grandfather, Raven mentioned the name Jonathan. On the tape you hear a male voice say, "Jonathan," right before she does.

Although we tried to contact the client for a follow-up interview, our calls were not returned. We feel confident in the fact that the grandfather will protect her and hope all has remained calm.

Evidence

We love getting evidence because it not only confirms what our mediums pick up, but also our clients have proof that they're not crazy!

Photos:
Jesus Picture With Face
Orbs In Bedroom

EVPs:
"Go Away"
"Edgar"
"And What Do You See?"

Personal Experiences:
After the clearing, Raven went to touch her camera and it closed before she could touch it.

Someone breathed in Katie's ear.

Raven felt like the air around her was heated.

Crew Afterthoughts

Raven: This house was one of the easiest to clear. There wasn't a lot of phenomena and only a few of the spirits were mildly negative. This is when I found out that spirits can make themselves apparent to only one medium. Through Beckah we were able to prevent the client's father from being cleared along with the other spirits.

Beckah: Being affected by a spirit is not always pleasant, but at least he got his message across and it helped the family to know that one of their own was around and protecting them to the best of his ability.

Katie: Honestly, I didn't feel a lot there, but I stayed downstairs with the client where as most of the activity was in the upstairs area. So that is kind of expected. However, I did feel something brush against my ear as if in passing when the whole group was together at the end of the investigation.

Geena's House

"Don't go upstairs!"

—EVP

In December, we were contacted by a woman who was at her wits end. She had a home with her two children and not a few ghosts. These ghosts made themselves known in spades. She'd had problems ever since she'd moved in and it had steadily gotten worse.

After having a very brief discussion, Ghost Quest decided it was time to step in. Raven, Beckah, Sandy, and Ben got in the car and headed over to Geena's house. They arrived to find a quaint looking country house with a large expanse of land adjoining it. This investigation just proved looks can be deceiving.

Upon entering the home, there was a feeling of anxiousness, heaviness, and activity—nothing within the home was still. The crew sat with Geena and had her recount once more what she was dealing with. One of the most telling signs were general feelings of discontent and anger among family members when there were no apparent arguments before they bought the property. This could be a result of the spirits or residual energy within the home.

She continued, "My daughter has seen an old woman in her room and a younger one as well. I have fixed things in the playroom only to find they are all disrupted when I go back upstairs. I get woken up in the middle of the night to loud noises and bangs. Like hearing walking across the floor, knocks and raps, objects being dragged upstairs, children giggling or crying. My blankets get pulled off me at night. I didn't know what to do or who to turn to; then I found you guys." The group reassured her that Ghost Quest would do all it could to help.

The investigation began and the mediums were immediately aware of a family who had previously lived on the property. They were both drawn to the fireplace in the den; here they saw scenes of a fire within the old home. They felt this was what had killed the family, and the death was not prolonged, hence the spirit remained.

In the kitchen, Raven made the crew aware of five spirits from the family that both psychics had felt were connected to the fire—a grandmother, a father, a mother, a daughter (two to four years old), and another daughter (seven to eight years of age). Aware of these spirits, the crew decided to venture upstairs, but upon touching the fourth step, it began to feel like we were hip deep in snow. Beckah and Raven both experienced heart racing and a crushing sensation within their chests. This impacted Raven so heavily she was immobilized for a few moments.

She then connected with Geena's grandmother, which the owner was excited to hear as they were both very close, and it was later confirmed she had died of heart complications. Usually, when our psychics connect to spirits, they feel physical ailments that are connected to the spirits. Once these feelings are acknowledged, the sensations dissipate. It is just one of the many forms of spirit communication.

Upon entering an upstairs bedroom, everyone could hear a child's soft moan. Raven continued to feel Geena's grandmother upstairs as well as the two- to four-year-old daughter who was shown to be responsible for the toys being moved.

At this point, Geena and Raven were in one of the bedrooms and saw the little girl playing behind the curtain that covers the closet. Geena saw the curtain moving back and forth. There were no drafts in the room. The crew descended downstairs after leaving a tape recorder in the bedroom to see if they could get more auditory phenomena.

Later they continued downstairs to the cellar where a heavy male presence could be found. This was not the father; this was another presence. The crew heard this man quietly talking, and as the group took pictures; his face was visible against a wall.

Ghost Quest attributed the cause of the disturbances mainly to the family of spirits that felt they were still running their home; the man who seemed to occupy the basement was a fairly quiet spirit.

Geena did not want our help with clearing the spirits. She was happy letting them live their afterlife within her home and to hear there was no intent to harm or scare her or her daughters.

Later, as the crew went through the EVPs, they discovered many audible occurrences that resulted from the family, Geena's grandmother, and the man downstairs. Everything the owner's family had been hearing was confirmed. There was not a lot of photographic evidence, but the man's face was by itself an extraordinary capture by the Ghost Quest crew.

All who participated within this investigation were pleased with the results and deemed the house wonderfully haunted!

Evidence

There have been cases we have dealt with that have a good amount of EVPs, but none that was so rude! Either way, though, we are happy with the evidence.

Photos:
Ectoplasm on the floor
Someone's in the mirror
Orbs in the bedroom

EVPs:
"Don't go upstairs"
"B--tch"
"Mama"
Giggle

Personal Experiences:
Raven felt crushing pain in her chest on the stairs and was unable to move.

Crew Afterthoughts

Raven: This house was creepy. You could feel the spirits as soon as you walked in. Hearing the baby cry in the upstairs bedroom was just weird. There were no negative spirits, just very active ones, and the families acceptance of what was happening was refreshing and good to see.

Beckah: The spirits were just all over the place during the investigation, and I felt like there was just no resting, every spirit was constantly busy. I could understand the client's unease at the level of activity within the home and was extremely happy to discover there were no negative presences.

Katie: I wasn't there but when I read the case file, it gave me the heebi jeebies!

Dudley Road

"Did you see that?"

—Katie

Dudley Road is an amazing place located in Massachusetts between a mix of older and newer residences; it looks like a typical suburban street. Except maybe near the end with a farmhouse that is half sunken into the ground and an sanitarium that has supposedly been abandoned for over fifty years (we cannot confirm this; it may just be part of the creep factor in the ghost stories told about the street) that still looks like it was opened yesterday and is still in use. It was suggested we visit such a unique area, so we did!

Ghost Quest investigators, Raven, Beckah, Katie, and Doug Warren drove down the narrow street. As soon as we saw the sanitorium set back from the road, we stopped. This was our first landmark; we knew we were near the hot spot of activity. When we got out of the car, we slowly walked down the road getting a feeling for the area, and it was an ominous feeling. We kept getting the impression that we were being watched and the closer we came to the sunken farmhouse the sicker we felt. We had never felt such heaviness in an open area.

Across the street from the sunken farm house, the energy was sizzling. Out of the corner of our eyes we saw figures running in the field and the feeling of being watched began to consume us. It was as though we were prey caught in the cross hairs of a hunter's rifle, and we knew there was no escape. Raven and Beckah immediately picked up the residual energy of violence in this quiet community—which is believed to confirm the local lore of a convent's slaughter at the hand of a mad man.

Man in third window at Dudley Road,
an abandoned insane asylum.

When we found the sunken farmhouse, we couldn't believe our eyes. Never had we seen such an odd sight; it was as
though the earth just swallowed it up to the second story. As
the light started to fade, we walked back toward the car to get
flashlights. When we got to the car by the sanitarium, horses
hooves could be heard rambling down the street. Armed with
flashlights, we walked back toward the field. The group stayed
together out of both fear and excitement.

About halfway there, Raven and Beckah yelped. Each
saying they heard growling from the woods on their left, we
decided to split up to see if this would make the spirits more
likely to contact us. As we reached the field again, it was pitch
black out; the group discussed the idea of breaking up into
groups. There were four of us, so Doug and Beckah headed
back to the sanitarium, leaving Raven and Katie down at the
field and sunken home.

As Doug and Beckah headed up to the asylum, we
snapped shots and were benefited with a light show. As we
stood outside the building's small gate, we could see movement inside the building, although the only car on this end
of the street was ours, and the doors were all locked. It may

have been an abandoned asylum, but it looked well kept and new. It added a little more mystery to our already obscure surroundings.

As we walked the street, each of us had an experience. It was extremely frightening and fun. When Doug and Beckah walked back to the group, we were greeted by a very freaked Katie and Raven. Our demonologist who claims, "I can handle standing toe to toe with a demon, but if I see a spirit ten feet away, I'll run like a little girl," had seen the animal that both Raven and Beckah had heard earlier. She said it was the size of a fox, but didn't have a bushy tail. Its fur was stringy and its eyes were a yellow color.

This could have been any number of animals native to the area, except that it was transparent. Katie had seen it by a tree and she could literally see through it to the stumps of trees behind. After the experience, she turned her back to the woods, not wanting to see it anymore. But she kept getting the feeling of being threatened or being grabbed, so she decided to stay in the middle of the street on neutral territory; there she wouldn't have to worry.

Beckah had been having reactions to the spirits and energy all night. On and off she would feel light headed and

White ectoplasm coming from Doug's flashlight by the clearing where the nuns were reportedly killed.

dizzy; at other times she would feel stomach sicknesses or have a headache. On the ride back was when the horror really started for her. It seems that one of the spirits that resided on the street had decided to hitch a ride home with us.

Beckah is a channel, and when her guard is down, she can sometimes be easily taken over. However, during this trip she did keep her guard up. But the spirit kept trying to psychically attack her, trying to get in. Beckah experienced horrifying visions of the spirit's past proving to her and her colleagues the truth behind the legend surrounding the area.

What Beckah received were images of the woman running and being stabbed, then her throat being slit. The spirit still saw herself this way and we could now all understand how people could get so freaked with spirits in that condition haunting the area. Beckah became so overwhelmed with the emotions and energy she almost fainted.

Raven stepped in to save the day clearing the car, and as she did that, Beckah heard screams from the woman or at least she thought it was the woman—but it was, in fact, the psychic herself. It seems as though the spirit was more attached to her than she thought. But all ended well.

Doug was not badly affected, but we did have a couple of photos taken of him with orbs and a white streak. There was one particularly fascinating photo of him with white ectoplasm coming from his flashlight. He did feel the heaviness everyone else did and saw the bodies moving in the sanitarium. Although he wasn't as affected, he did later confess the energy made him feel a little lightheaded.

Raven was affected in multiple ways, from feeling dizzy, to hearing dog growlings. She felt consistently that she saw figures out of the corners of her eyes, although she did not open herself to tapping into the spirits. She felt they were too violent.

Turns out her intuition was right on, as proven by the experiences on the ride back. Raven also experienced an all-natural phenomenon within our rural surroundings. She was bitten by a spider! But two months later the spider bites still had not left or healed—in fact, they got deeper. It took a trip to the dermatologist to find out it was a specific type of spider bite whose venom attacks skin cells. To this day, Raven has deep scars on

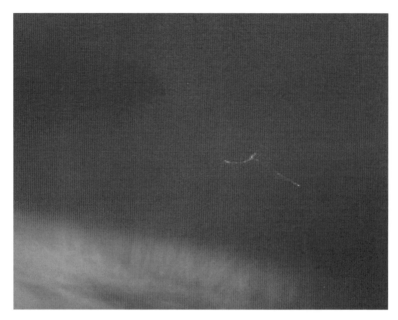

A light streak by the car on Dudley Road.

Orbs in upper right corner.

her leg where the bites were, a daily reminder of her trip to the mystifying Dudley Road.

For all of Dudley Roads scary times, Ghost Quest holds a deep remorse for the spirits there. We wish we could help them. Unfortunately, we feel that if we opened ourselves up to doing so, we would instead be attacked. We hope one day, we may develop a way to safely give them their release into the peace and harmony of the afterlife.

Evidence

Lots of evidence on this case; we were all excited that the spirits decided to really show themselves!

Photos:
Energy ropes

Lights going through trees along the road where the nuns were killed.

Mist in the dale
Flashlight ectoplasm

EVPs:
Growl
Horses Trotting

Personal Experiences:
There were no other personal experiences felt during this case.

History of Dudley Road, Billerica

❖ The town of Billerica was settled in 1638 and it actually holds one of the best preserved Native American burial sites dating back to one thousand B.C.

❖ Three nuns from Daughters of Saint Paul were hung along Dudley Road after being accused of witchcraft.

❖ A few who had escaped hanging were hunted down and their throats were slit.

❖ The house they had resided in is reported to have sunk into the ground up to the second story.

❖ A little bit off the street lies an abandoned insane asylum; however, if this is the same place we saw, it still looks new.

Another light streak.

Crew Afterthoughts

Raven: Dudley Road was just overwhelming with the amount of activity we were seeing. From hearing the horses, watching Beckah being affected by one of the spirits, to seeing all the orbs and light anomalies made this an investigation to remember. I can't wait to go back!

Beckah: Dudley Road was phenomenal, all the audible and physical phenomena was just impressive! It was scary and fun.

Katie: It was awesome! That's a place that is on my top ten to visit. It had scary and tragic history, but what an eergized place.

House through the trees is the sunken farm house where the nuns supposedly resided before their deaths.

Pine Hill Cemetery
(A.K.A. Blood Cemetery)

"Behold my friends as you pass by, as you are now so once was I. As I am now so you will be. Prepare for death and follow me."

—Written on a gravestone

By this point in Ghost Quest, we had developed biweekly meetings with much coffee (thank you Rayna). We were discussing upcoming investigations when one of the members related a tale about Abel Blood and his very hellish headstone. In local lore, it is told that Abel Blood murdered his family and that his headstone had a finger that pointed up towards heaven. But at night, it pointed down towards hell.

We decided on the spot that this was a place we needed to investigate, so we packed into our cars and began our expedition. Armed with directions, we went in search of the cemetery, however, it seemed the spirits that night just did not want us there. We passed the cemetery at least three times, lost the road twice, and had to make a stop for another cup of coffee. This was but the first of many odd experiences in this exciting and creepy cemetery.

Upon entering Blood Cemetery, the first thing everyone noticed was the absence of winds and drastic temperature differences between the street and the property. Katie, Beckah, Sandy, Raven, and Doug started toward the back of the cemetery. Sandy and Raven became nauseated upon entering Pine Hill and it increased as they traveled to the back of the cemetery. Sandy and Raven decided to stay towards the center where the sensations were not so heavy. Beckah and Katie continued on. The always intrepid Katie went immediately into search mode. She, together with Beckah, took off darting straight to the back wall. Katie went over looking for the notorious Blood house, which was supposedly located on Pine Hill near the cemetery.

On the other side of the wall she noticed the temperature returned to normal as did the winds. There were no other abnormalities to be seen or felt and she returned to the dead air that is Blood Cemetery. Katie and Beckah then began to look for the headstone of Abel Blood. It was easily found, smack dab in the middle of the cemetery, however, there were two of them. One Abel Blood died in 1862 at the age of fifty-six, the other died in 1870 (?) at the age of seventy. Good thing local legend told us about the finger because only the fifty-six-year-old Abel had it.

We found our man and began calling out to him; on our tape, it seemed only when we asked for him to talk did the wind pick up in what was otherwise a calm area. There was nothing outside of the tape to convince us Abel still haunted the cemetery.

In the meantime, Doug was exploring the left wall in the woods which seemed measurably darker. He kept feeling like someone was walking along the edge of the wall, watching the group. Fairly freaked, Doug walked back to the group and explained what he felt. Unfortunately, it was never fully explored. With everyone back in the cemetery, the real ghost hunting began. Tape recorders were set about and digital cameras went to work—yes, we were a primitive ghost hunting group... then.

Sandy was walking around with a tape recorder as Raven connected with a male spirit that was present. At this time Beckah had sat at a grave and looked up only to realize the name on the grave was the same as her own, "Rebecca." More than a little freaked, she got up and began inspecting other graves. She read aloud inscriptions so she could transcribe them later. There were a couple of memorable ones such as, "Dry up your tears surviving friends, mourn not for me but for your sins. Dead to the world, live unto God for the grave must soon be your abode." or "Behold my friends as you pass by, as you are now so once was I. As I am now so you must be. Prepare for death and follow me."

As Beckah read these morbid inscriptions on the tape, you can hear both male and female voices mumbling in the background. She had been bent down at on particular grave where the inscription was covered in dirt; as you hear her scraping, trying to read the words, you can easily make out a male voice saying, "Open your shirt up!" Beckah made no note of hearing a male voice at the time, and but oddly after the voice, she states, "It's so cold right here, I'm going to get frostbite, but I don't care."

After more mumbling from both her and the spirits, she finally gave up and found the rest of the group. Sandy then gave Raven the tape recorder. At one point, Katie was drawn to a small non-descript headstone, weather beaten and un-named. She felt a negative energy around it and called Raven over, who confirmed Katie's feelings.

As we traveled row by row, we ended up back at the front of the cemetery where we found a white headstone dating back to 1893. As Katie and Beckah looked closer, we realized that the earth was torn up just at the edge where the headstone met the grass. Upon uncovering the small hole, we found some coin, as if in offering. Noticing we were not with the rest of the group, we stood up and got ready to walk back when we realized a quarter had materialized on top of the headstone. Out of what Beckah and Katie felt was respect, we placed two quarters on either side of the materialized coin and left to go back to the rest of the crew who were gathered around Raven.

She was hunched over hands on her knees, and she kept quietly repeating, "I'm sick, I'm sick." Slowly, with labored breath, she stood upright. She decided then it would be best to make a retreat for the cars, knowing if a spirit had the ability to make her feel that horrible, it could most likely do worse to others.

Our team quickly did just that; we talked excitedly as we walked to the cars, in part because of the phenomena, and partly out of fear. If there were ghosts behind us, at this point, we didn't want to know.

Upon reaching the cemetery gate, we all noticed the air shift; autumn was around us once again, wind whipped through the trees, and a chill made us pull our coats tighter around. We all breathed a sigh of relief to be out of the cemetery. But gluttons for punishment that we were, we couldn't wait to have another go.

Back at GQHQ, there were many remarkable EVPs and photos. Just before Beckah had sat at the grave that bared her name, a young woman whispered, "Don't sit." As Sandy walked with the tape recorder, heavy breathing and a male voice could be heard mumbling something. When Sandy handed the tape recorder to Raven, a male voice said, "I'm sooooo cold!" These coupled with some wonderful pictures give proof that Blood Cemetery is very haunted!

Evidence

There were lots of unexpected evidence, and we were all surprised by the EVP evidence!

Photos:
Orbs and mists

EVPs:
"Open your shirt up"
"I'm so..co...cold"
"Whatever you say"
Whispering and mumbling
"Don't Sit"

Personal Experiences:
Raven and Sandy felt sick. Doug felt as though he was being watched.

**Fiction and Facts Of Pine Hill Cemetery
(A.K.A Blood Cemetery)**

❖ The land for Pine Hill Cemetery was generously donated to the young town of Hollis by Mr. Benjamin Parker Jr. when he sold the farm in the 1760s.

❖ Many of the founding families of Hollis are buried there.

❖ Due to the huge amount of damage from weather and age, many of the headstones are now unmarked.

❖ There are two sets of Blood headstones, one a set of two and the other a set of seven, and all are related to Abel.

❖ It has been said that late at night the finger that points up on Abel Bloods headstone turns and points the way down to Hell.

❖ Another legend is that the Blood family were all murdered on the same night. This is a fallacy as all the headstones have different dates of death.

Crew Afterthoughts

Raven: Blood cemetery…well…um…not my most favorite place to visit. Mostly because of the nauseous feeling that I got there. I get that frequently with negative places, but it was far more intense there. I would go back again, though.

Beckah: Pine Hill Cemetery was a delight! The tombstones which dated back to the 1700s had some of the most beautiful scriptures, and the legends surrounding the place lived up to my expectations completely!

Katie: I would like to go back again and find the Plague House. It was a very interesting burial site with a lot of history that was fun to explore.

Meredith's House

"Where's the monster?"

—Sean

Ghost Quest got a frantic phone call from a beleaguered woman. It seems this woman's six-year-old son was in touch with a questionable spirit. The boy was found playing in the cellar, and when asked what he was doing, stated that he was playing with the "monster." The cellar, although repeatedly warned against it, was a favored hangout for Sean and his otherworldly playmate. He often stated that his friend was sleeping, or would point up to the ceiling to show his mother where it was hiding. He spent almost a year and a half playing with this entity and causing the mother to question her son's mental health, until she was told by a close friend to call us.

Upon arriving, we began talking with the woman and soon discovered that she had to tried reach out to someone before but was unable to receive any real assistance. We were faced with someone who needed a little compassion, a friendly ear, and a helping hand. We met her son Sean, who played us beautiful melodies all throughout our investigation on his harmonica. He's an energetic six year old, but for the past year or so he had taken to hanging out in the basement with his friend "the monster," This entity seemed to follow Sean around the house but was rooted in the cellar. He would point up at the ceiling and exclaim, "The monster is sleeping!" In his bedroom, the closet door was a mirror and he would see the monster in the reflection watching him fall asleep.

As the interview wound down, we asked Sean to show us where the monster lived; immediately (with harmonica in hand), he took us to the basement entrance and looked at his mom, making sure it was okay to descend the stairs. We turned on all of our tape recorders and cameras prepared for a fascinating hunt.

There was an open bulkhead that helped circulate fresh air into the well-lit basement. However, there was the typical heaviness that we encounter all the time when spirits are active, and a slight smell. We watched Sean carefully make his way to the darkest area of the basement. There were fluorescent lights all around, but they seemed not to touch this one section. He stood next to the washer and dryer and pointed directly across from them. On the wall opposite, was an old dresser. This didn't interest us; what was beside the dresser, however, caught Katie's attention right away. As she gazed into the mirror, she saw faces—inhuman faces. We now knew for certain where Sean's friend lived. Evidently, he had invited others to play too. Katie felt the mirror was a hideaway, not a portal; the entities were trapped.

Raven knew that with the demonic entities had come some negative spirits. She sensed them around her, and like the others, the spirits were rooted in the basement. Katie and Raven decided to commence with the clearing. Beckah took Sean and Meredith upstairs, so the mother and son would be out of harms way. She was an experienced energy cleanser and began a cleansing of Sean and the mother, so there would be no residual energy left on them or the house.

Downstairs, Raven and Katie discussed battle plans as they kept an eye on the mirror, knowing that if the entities came out, all hell would break loose. As we watched, the mirror began to fog up. Katie knew what was coming, and quickly put a binding seal on the four corners of each side of the mirror, preventing the entities from leaving their hidey hole. Katie continued to watch the mirror warily, however. She said, "I'm not feeling any fighting or anything. It's like they already gave up. They're smart." She then drew more complex seals on the mirror, binding them inside for an eternity.

Safe in the knowledge that the demonic entities were sealed away and could not interfere, Raven began clearing the negative spirits. She stood aggressively in the middle of the basement, calling out to them, telling them they must leave. When there was no response and feeling of release, she quickly called in her Higher Beings and ancestors for assistance. She began to chant, "Take them away, take them away!" She watched the entities struggle. After roughly ten minutes, the negative spirits had been subdued and removed from the house.

Raven called for the family and Beckah to come downstairs. Sean was twice asked, "Where is the monster?" He only answered with a shake of his head. However, on the tape you can hear a male spirit with a rushed grainy voice saying, "I'm here." The child became agitated over the loss of his friend and demanded a search. So Beckah dutifully walked with him all around the cellar, out the bulkhead, and around the property. When Beckah returned, Sean was full of excitement yelling for his mom. When he finally got Meredith's attention he said, "Monster all gone!" Then he asked if he could go back outside. As he asks, we hear on the tape, "Outside," in that same rushed male voice.

Although neither Raven or Beckah picked up on the spirit, Katie who was left downstairs to seal the basement's exits and entrances began to have doubts about the success of the clearing. As she was about to seal the bulkhead door, her Holy Water was thrown from her hand. She quickly picked it up and began sprinkling it around the area. At the same time, the fluorescent lights flashed on and off with a loud hiss. She came to the conclusion that one spirit had gotten away, but knew he would not be able to get back in the house and she was not worried.

We left the house. Katie had taken possession of the mirror, to keep it away from curious eyes and hands. When we returned to headquarters and went over the tapes, we also realized that when Sean stood at the basement entrance, that same male voice could be heard calling his name. Not a second after, you hear his little feet clopping down the steps. Although one spirit had gotten away, we felt the clearing thoroughly successful. Even Meredith had commented on how much brighter the area where the mirror had been was, and that there was a peace in the basement.

Two weeks later, we received another frantic call from Meredith. She said Sean was now gravitating toward her garage, and when she would pull up in her car at night, she got the distinct feeling of being threatened. We decided to go back and help the family.

The garage, a separate building from the house, looks like a barn. When Raven got out of her car, she saw (right away), a spirit walk into the carport and knew that one had escaped from the clearing held at our last investigation. We knew that this particular one tipped Katie's Holy Water and caused the activity with the lights. *This* time, the entity would not get away. Although it was not the demonic entities Katie had dealt with in the home; it was a very negative spirit. We thought that when the spirit escaped, he would have gone to another location—not stay on the property or make camp in the garage.

No clearing is uneventful. We had our audio recorders rolling and our cameras were flashing. Meredith and Sean decided to stay within the home, although her son did try to come out and "play" with the spirit a few times. Raven at this time tried to communicate with the entity, and although the spirit did not speak, he revealed his open hostility to her, making her feel uncomfortable and unwanted. This was not a new feeling for Raven when it came to clearings; many spirits already know why you are coming before you get there, and this spirit was prepared for her. Refusing to leave, and squatting in a corner, Raven approached him and proceeded to participate in a tug of war with the spirit. For over fifteen minutes this continued; eventually Raven won out and the negative presence dissipated. The crew returned to the home and told Meredith all was well.

We have kept in contact with Meredith, and she has made a recent move south, although she assures us it was for love and not due to any kind of haunting. We wish her the best in her new home.

The photographs were non-descript but the EVPs were thrilling—growls and inexplicable whooshing sounds pervaded the tapes.

Evidence

There was some good evidence in this case, it was obvious from the first interview we had that it wasn't going to be easy to clear the home.

Photos:
  Entities in the mirror
  White streak in garage
  Orbs in cellar

EVPs:
  "Robbie!"
  "Outside."
  "I'm here!"
  Growling

Personal Experiences:
  Katie's Holy Water bottle was knocked from her hand, lights flickered on and off. Upstairs while the clearing was going on, Sean became highly agitated.

Crew Afterthoughts

Raven: Meredith's house was a hard investigation, mostly because of the young son being used by the spirit. He didn't understand why the monster went away. My heart went out to him for that reason. Otherwise, it was a good job done...twice!

Beckah: This case is very close to me; whenever a child is involved, I want to do everything I can to protect them from the dangers that spirits can bring with them. Concerning the fact that we weren't dealing with just spirits and, in fact, inhuman entities made me doubly protective.

Katie: I won't forget this case. It was a little hairy for a moment, when the holy water was flung out of my hand. When I came home with the mirror, I could see the entities inside. I counted five in all. It's an amazing item. The mirror is now in special storage, and a cloth is always covering the mirror.

Dearborn Hall

A very stressed building owner who was renovating a large building called in the Ghost Quest crew. The changes to the building were causing a huge amount of paranormal phenomena to occur. The building was a late 1800s brick three-story; the top floor was the most active at the time and when the Ghost Quest investigators went on a daytime walk-through, they came across a heaviness similar to other places they had checked out.

First stop was downstairs in the finished game room. Here there have been instances of seeing a man, orbs, and a feeling of being watched, which some members of the crew also felt.

As they climbed up to the second story, the heaviness on the stairs increased as if they were wading through mud or snow. They noticed as they stepped onto the second floor landing that, even though there were many large windows here, there was a distinct absence of light that one would expect to filter through the building. After walking through the offices on this floor, they stopped to give the owner a chance to ask some questions. Beckah immediately felt like she was being led quickly up the stairs, and said as much to Raven. Raven told her to go with it, once she was given free reign to go where she was being taken. Raven and the crew followed.

A picture was taken of Beckah as she ascended the stairs. In front of her stands a man looking back, as if to make sure she and the crew are following. When we arrived at the top floor, it was apparent the owner was still in the middle of renovations, as tools and supplies were evident.

As you walked in, the first thing you noticed, aside from the tools, were the two large half-circle stages on either side of the room. The walls behind them were each painted by

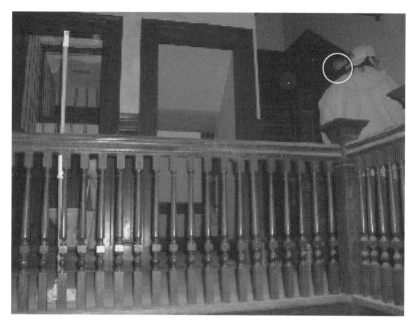

Beckah being "led" up the stairs by an apparition.

the owner. One wall depicted a beautiful grand piano, the other a Grecian vase holding long vines and delicate flowers. The musty smell permeated the air as did the feeling of the history that surrounded the building. The heaviness on this floor was thick as well, alerting us to the fact that there were many spirits not at rest here.

As the crew walked deeper into the room, we noticed that there was a large antique bank safe, which could only be removed by a helicopter because it weighed over one thousand pounds. It was a marvel in itself. We were also made aware of a hidden spot in the floor; a small door opened and revealed a cubby hole where we were told there was Nazi paraphernalia as well as papers concerning a gentleman's club. We came to the conclusion the two were connected due to the time frame the owner gave us for both documents. Unfortunately, she did not keep them in the building and we were not able to get copies.

After a while, looking about the room and getting a feel for the spirits, the crew, except Katie, continued on to investigate the other two rooms on the top floor. Beckah decided to investigate the office on the right. On the door to the office, there was an old-fashioned peep hole with a gold disk that slid and covered the hole. The spirits decided to play and began to move the disk; Beckah tweaked and booked, found Raven, and rejoined the group. Raven's interest was peaked and she and the owner went over to check out the door. It was just as Beckah described, and there was no way the disk could have slipped, as a lever had to be moved in order to open the hole. Raven was impressed, but even more so when they got back to GQHQ. On the tape, you could hear the click of the disk sliding into place and Beckah tweaking. Meanwhile, Katie was in the ominous main room feeling as though she was being prevented from leaving. Oddly enough, the usually observant crew did not notice Katie was not with them. Nor did they look for her. Although we were on the same floor and Katie repeatedly yelled for someone to come, no one heard a sound. During that time, she felt the heaviness, but nothing threatening. When the group finally found her, a picture was taken of her and she was literally covered in orbs.

With that bit of drama behind them, the crew descended the stairs to see what they could find on the second floor. The first thing they saw was a piano from which the owner took

Orbs in the main ballroom.

inspiration. This baby grand was also original to the building's occupants. On closer inspection, a crew member pointed out the tiny fingerprints lying in the dust on the keys. When they asked the owner if she had any children here recently, she advised that the only place the children went was the first floor, as it was a fully finished game room. She'd had the stairs roped off, and no one except herself and her husband would have been upstairs.

Curious, Raven decided to take a picture of the piano and the remnants of its tiny player. An orb was seen laying on the keys covering the tiny fingerprints. Not soon after, in the EVPs, piano playing can be heard.

While the other members were taken with the piano, the owner wanted to talk to Raven privately. As they were talking, Raven looked down the hall at the door to one of the other offices. On the door appeared the face of a man in his late thirties or early forties. It was only his head and he was smiling. They watched the face as it slowly disappeared.

The crew regrouped in the first floor game room. Night was descending and they needed to get their game plan in order for the evening's events. Much like most well-laid plans, their's soon went awry. They decided that after a short break they would once more head upstairs to the third floor. They all felt ready and eager for this part of the investigation to commence.

In the doorway of the main room they all noticed that the heaviness had increased dramatically. Once inside the room, it seemed to diminish a bit. They all took seats that surrounded the platform and waited for Beckah and Raven to tap in to the energies there. Raven began to look distressed, and when Beckah asked what was wrong, Raven said she felt like she was having a heart attack. She somehow knew it was a spirit attack and asked for someone to escort her downstairs. Beckah nodded to Sandy and gave her a look that said, "Make sure she's okay."

While they remained downstairs, Raven noted that her symptoms lessened. Sandy did make an attempt to clear Raven, but it was unsuccessful and the symptoms started coming back. At that point, Sandy ran upstairs to get Katie. Katie came down and asked Raven what was going on. Raven told her she had two or three spirits with her and that she could feel them. She also told Katie that they didn't want her here. Katie nodded, knowing what needed to be done, and by the time it was over, she'd removed three spirits from the medium. Because Raven had been previously attacked, Beckah thought she would be more susceptible and asked Katie to stay downstairs so she wouldn't be affected while Beckah was channeling. Raven agreed and the channeling session began.

Upstairs, on the quest for more history about the building, Beckah began the session. She took a seat on one of the small platforms in the main third floor room, and attempted to connect with the spirits around her. A spirit named Jessica came through Beckah, taking over her motor skills and her speech.

Jessica was about thirty-four years old when she passed and had a tragic history. The owner proceeded to grill the spirit about the bank safe that could not be opened. Unfortunately, this particular spirit could offer her no help, but did make them aware of the fact that she had lost two children and felt it was due to people of her time. When the owner would not stop questioning the spirit, instead of just letting her say her piece, the spirit became more irate.

The spirit proceeded to run downstairs wailing into the main floor and began to pace back and forth across the room like a caged animal. Raven then approached the spirit within Beckah's body and told her everything was going to be okay, and that Beckah needed to let go of the spirit. When the spirit receded, Raven hugged Beckah until she finished crying for the loss Jessica suffered, which felt so much like it was her own.

With everyone returning to the main room, the crew deemed the investigation over. The car ride home was a wonderful event as everyone rehashed what had happened. They were eager to go over the evidence. After thoroughly reviewing each picture and each of the three tapes, they came up with overwhelming evidence to support the owner's belief that the building was extremely haunted!

During follow-up the owner related that she had decided against a clearing, and Ghost Quest returned to headquarters to look over the evidence.

Evidence

There was quite a bit of evidence, and we were all excited that the client got the confirmation they need.

Photos:
Orbs everywhere!
Face in third floor window.
Orb on the piano along with tiny fingerprints.
Beckah during channeling had two sets of arms and legs.

EVPs:
"Wait"
Piano Playing
Lots of whispering

Personal Experiences:
There were no other personal experiences felt during this case.

Historical Facts About Dearborn Hall

❖ Built in August 29, 1908, it is 4 stories and 16,280 sq. ft.
❖ Before it was sold to the current owner, it was given away twice for absolutely nothing.
❖ The appraisal price for the building is $1,125,600. It was sold in 1998 for one quarter the cost to the current owner... hmmm, wonder why?
❖ The Independent Order of the Odd Fellows once resided within the building. The Odd Fellows were created in the idea that common laboring men should band together to form a fraternity for social unity and fellowship. In the eighteenth century, when they came together, the notion of helping others was uncommon and so the members became known as "peculiar" or "odd," hence they were derided as "Odd Fellows."
❖ He was into the business of hardware and worked for both Daniels & Co., then for John B. Varick, the two largest hardware places in the late nineteenth and early

The Dearborn Building as it stands today. It is privately owned.

twentieth century. George became widely acquainted in church and lodge circles, and was a member of the Ridgely Lodge of Odd Fellows. A Republican, he was several times elected to the school board, and, in 1887, was elected to represent his ward in the State Legislature. He was known for his "fearless speech." (Webmaster, Joe Labbe, of www. goffesfalls.org collected this information; see resource page.)

❖   George W. Dearborn's wife died in 1906, and it would seem that it was her will that provided for the building of the Oak Hill Lodge (Dearborn Memorial Hall) I.O.O.F. (Independent Order of Odd Fellows). She built the Hall in memoriam of George. (Webmaster, Joe Labbe, of www.goffesfalls.org collected this information; see resource page.)

Crew Afterthoughts

Raven: The Dearborn building was an experience and a half—right up there with Devil's Church. It was scary for me because I really felt like I was having a heart attack, and being a large woman, that is completely feasible. Thanks to Katie for her quick thinking! Also watching Beckah go through the possession was intense. It's hard to watch someone go through all that. All in all, I would love to get back in there and investigate with the equipment we have now. It would be a hell of an experience, no pun intended.

Beckah: I will never forget this building and the spirits that lie within it. It was the first time I consciously channeled a spirit, and I can still feel what that spirit felt. Hearing the piano play was just amazing, and Katie being stuck in a room was just a fabulous piece of phenomena. The fact that we never heard her… that just shows the strength of the spirits in the building.

Katie: It was an odd experience. I've never been stuck in a room before; it really felt like someone was holding me in. The interior of the building was marvelous, with a lot of nooks and crannies that I was just dying to investigate. It seemed as though orbs literally covered the cameras no matter where we went. I'm just upset no one noticed I was missing… hello?

Cavalry Cemetery

"I'm so co…cold."

—Spirit

From the outside, Cavalry Cemetery is both quiet and beautiful. A serene spot holds the children's graves, guarded by a bronze angel who is heard singing at night. Lush grasses and sprawling pines make this graveyard seem like a calm and welcoming site to travel.

Ghost Quest believed this investigation would be relaxing compared to the other cases we had recently been involved in. We walked amongst the magnificently carved headstones, both old and new. A feeling of peace descended as we traveled toward the back of the cemetery watching the sky glow pink and the sunset.

When we reached the center of the cemetery, we noticed an immediate temperature spike—although there was a slight spring heat, the difference was amazing and set us on alert. As we stood upon the hill and looked down at the beautiful bronze angel, the children's plot, and the other graves that lined the woods behind them, our feeling of serenity was broken as the caws of a hundred crows filled the sky.

Looking to the trees, we saw the culprits staring back at us as if in warning. As we continued forward, the crows calls became more erratic and insistent. We all began to feel as if we were uninvited guests at a dinner party with everyone telling us to leave. Immediately, Katie our occult sciences expert and demonologist, began to feel a dark energy lingering by the woods. Without saying a word, she went to explore the tree line. The closer she got, the more she realized a summoning had occurred at some time around this area. With her ability to see inhuman spirits, she scanned the area looking for the meaning in the crow's warnings.

Unlike most of the crew, Raven felt the impact of the negative energy before we went through the gates and knew something was up, but decided not to go into it until everyone could discern their own feelings. As we gathered in the near dark by the tree line, Raven looked into the void of the forest and realized something was looking back. As the she hesitantly described the creature she was seeing to a fellow investigator, she talked of a six-to-seven-foot tall spirit with arms down to his knees and big yellow razor teeth, covered with hair.

Beckah who had visited Cavalry on a whim once before was not surprised by what the crew was suggesting they saw. She had her own experiences—evidence consisting of a large animal reflected in her car hood and window. Unfortunately, there was no animal to be seen, but Beckah could be heard clearly on the tape she had taken saying, "Oh my goodness! Do you see that!?" That is what she later describes as an eight-to-ten-foot tall being with short arms and a hairless gremlin-like appearance, with a wide mouth and short pointed teeth.

When Katie meandered further into the woods, she knew we were not alone and got psychic images of a girl writing occult symbols in the dirt and raising inhuman spirits. She knew exactly what the girl was practicing, rejoined the group, and filled them in on what she'd discovered. This was not just any haunted spot, this area was demonically infested on purpose. The girl in her vision practiced what Katie called Black Earth. It is the practice of tapping into the oldest forms of black magick and using them to expand occult knowledge and open gateways to new planes of negative energy and creation. Through this process the girl had opened several gates that allowed demonic entities to travel back and forth.

With our demonologist investigating the treeline, we continued our investigations. Raven and Beckah also picked up on a female black-robed figure crouched near the ground, and Beckah felt portals all around. She muttered under her breath, "What the hell did she do here?"

With one recorder left near the angel so we could catch her singing, we also situated two other recorders along the

An orb in the right hand corner and a light streak by the angel.

tree line and one atop a headstone as a control, so we could distinguish actual paranormal phenomena from everyday disturbances.

We became frustrated at what seemed to the eye to be lack of visible paranormal phenomena. However, when attempting to take pictures, the camera's batteries seemed dry, for which there was no explanation as we had just put in fresh batteries before we left. We returned to the car for new batteries, and again had the same issue, so Fred decided maybe it was a bad batch of batteries and went off to get more.

As darkness descended, the uneasiness grew worse. An overwhelming paranoia-like feeling claimed us. We had no explanation for this, although we did feel like we needed to tread carefully as we were being closely watched and silently threatened. Although there was a heat, there were no bugs or animals to be heard or felt; the crows at some point had decided we were beyond help, and there were no signs of our loud friends.

More orbs.

As Fred drove up with new batteries, we immediately closed in on him, feeling safer now that everyone was back together. With energy and sanity returned, we descended upon the area once again. Still technical troubles pervaded our case, cameras turned on and off by themselves, and as we checked on the tapes, they seemed to have turned themselves off.

It became obvious that the spirits did not want to be seen or heard. Katie instructed the crew not to hold vigils or call out, as the entities were already leery of us, and to ask them to do something trivial such as turning on a light would be interpreted as disrespect and could result in bodily harm. Katie compared Calvary to *Jurassic Park*, and reinforced the protections we use before we enter into any paranormal situation, because as she said, "There is always a hole in the electric fence."

We figured this would be all we were going to get this night, so we headed back to the headquarters to review the evidence. The photographs were phenomenal! Orbs, mists, and distorted faces ran through each photo; none lacked evidence. Upon the recordings we heard a male voice; it sounded as if he were frightened and agitated, but we heard his words clearly, "Cold…I'm so cold." As you hear Raven discussing the entity she was seeing to a fellow investigator, you hear a soft, almost warning, growl around her. There were a mix of demonic and human spirits speaking into the tapes and our control picked up nothing but a couple of planes passing by, which oddly enough, none of the other tapes recorded.

Evidence

There was a LOT of evidence for this case. We've gone back a few times since this first case and we've gotten even more!

Photos:
Orbs
Light strings
Blue mists

EVPs:
Growling
Footsteps—on tape left alone; no one was near it

Personal Experiences:
Katie and Beckah both saw demonic entities; Raven felt sickened. Beckah got headaches.

Cavalry Historical Facts

❖ A man named Father Halde who was the pastor at Ste. Marie founded Mount Saint Cavalry Cemetery in 1881.

The view looking down into where the practitioner raised her demons.

❖ The church built the cemetery around the belief of being raised with Christ, and it is of the Roman Catholic faith.

❖ From 1900-1922 over fifty acres was added to the cemetery as well as a receiving tomb, and it now takes up almost three blocks.

There is not much history for the area in which we investigated, however, if you would like more information please look to the back of the book for the Cavalry Cemetery website.

Crew Afterthoughts

Raven: Mount St. Calvary is one of the oddest places we have gone. This was my first glimpse into physically seeing dark creatures—okay, one dark creature, but still one is enough for a life time, and yet still I go back. Glutton for punishment I think. The nice thing here is where there is dark there is light, and that also is very evident. Calvary, very odd but very cool.

Beckah: I had been to Cavalry before and knew of the things that lived there. It felt almost like we were in *Jurassic Park* and the dinosaurs were loose. Threatening, beautiful, and scary as hell!

Katie: It was a unique case as usually when I find out that someone was summoning inhuman entities, the summoner is still present. This was a whole different *can of worms* because the person who practiced the occult and opened these portals is long gone. Usually, the practitioners blood is used to keep the gates opened and protected from others meddling. Unfortunately, this means only the one who opened the gateways can close them, and I don't think we will be finding out who it was anytime soon.

Unknown Litchfield Cemetery

"Use my energy to manifest."
—Raven

Off a little side road in Litchfield, three of the Ghost Quest crew, Raven, Doug, and Fred, went in search of some eerie experiences. Rumor had it that this cemetery was highly active and definitely deserved closer inspection. At sunset we took off to embark on our journey. An uneasy excitement filled us on the drive up and only worsened as we entered the wrought iron gates. To the eye, this small cemetery seemed rather lifeless, no pun intended, and boring, but we were soon to find we had bitten off perhaps more than we could chew.

When we first entered the graveyard, it was darker than on the drive up. The sky was turning to a dark blue and the sun could not be seen, but bats filled the skies creating a cloud over the cemetery. We stood for a short time in wonder, watching these little furry beings fly and dive over our heads, beginning their nighttime feasting. Doug began to walk the perimeter of the property feeling for energy and possible portals. Raven and Fred soon followed snapping pictures as we traveled, Raven, the medium, could feel presences within the confines of the cemetery, but did not feel that they were openly active like some of our other cases. However, her opinion soon changed, and we realized as it got darker, that the spirits got stronger.

As Raven continued to walk the grounds, she began to pick up on a female spirit, but the ghost was resistant to talk. However Fred, who is highly sensitive and empathic, was getting the feelings of a heart attack. The area where we were situated was all contrasting shadows; it was dark and eerie, giving you the impression that there were spirits all around you. Raven continued on her own path, but she noticed Fred cringing and grabbing his chest. As she realized his distress,

One lonely orb.

she looked around to find Doug, spotting him across the cemetery. As she laid her hand on Fred's back, whispering assurances, Doug spotted the happenings and ever so calmly sauntered over to the pair.

Together Doug and Raven removed Fred from the area and brought him to the center of the cemetery. Raven was disappointed that there wasn't much for spirit phenomena and began doubting all the stories she had been told. She began to think maybe she'd come on the wrong day, or maybe the stories were a little exaggerated.

Then an idea hit the medium. She decided to see what would happen if she allowed the spirits to draw off her energy. Maybe, she thought, because they spent so much energy every night, that they were just *pooped* tonight **(Ghost Quest encourages you to NEVER do this—it will cause things to happen, but it is not worth the physical consequences)**. It seems the spirits heard her loud and clear. She didn't feel anything, but orbs began to manifest in front of her photos. During this time, as the spirits were siphoning energy off of

Headstones.

Raven, she also got mists and neon bright beings. She could not believe her eyes, but as these wonderful manifestations were occurring, the side effects were starting to show.

Raven began to feel very shaky, dizzy, and knew if she didn't sit down, she would fall down. She let the rest of us know of her issues and we expressed our concern, mentioning the idea of leaving. After just beginning to get evidence, she wasn't about to leave! She squashed the idea right away and said she was just going to go to the car and recoup for a couple minutes; she would be right back. As Raven sat in the car, she created a psychic shield around herself so that the spirits would not get anymore of her energy. Doug and Fred continued to carry on the quest, Raven on our minds, as we looked over the headstones.

As we wandered the graveyard, Fred began to get the heart attack symptoms again—although they had lessened, the pain had never gone away completely. Even though he wasn't at the spot where it began, Fred got the feeling he was being followed. This began to intensify. He rubbed his chest, hoping the pain would dissipate, but it did not.

Opposite page:
After Raven asked for the spirits to draw off
her energy, she began to get mists.

While Fred suffered, Doug was all wrapped up in the energies. He could feel spirits around him and feel the energy they created—it was very intense and he became absorbed in it, trying to sense where exactly they manifested from.

Unfortunately, Fred's pain and Raven's reaction discouraged further investigation, and after Doug helped his colleague, we made the decision to leave the cemetery and the spirits for another day.

We left the area thinking of all we had seen and experienced. Doug decided to snap a couple of last pictures. It was littered with hundreds of orbs, as if the spirits were escorting us out. Feeling thoroughly unwelcome, we got to the car and headed home.

Evidence

There was very little hard evidence during this case. Below is a listing of evidence that we got.

Photos:
Orbs all over the place
Mists—after Raven asked them to use her energy to manifest

EVPs:
There was no electronic voice phenomena.

Personal Experiences:
Raven felt shaky after asking spirits to use her energy. Fred felt as though he was having heart attack.

As Fred and Doug left, it was as though the spirits were escorting them out.

Crew Afterthoughts

Raven: Little cemetery…HUGE amount of spirits! This cemetery is a great place to get evidence. I really learned a lesson that day. Never, ever tells spirits to use your energy, or at least put a cap on it. I will never do that again, but oh, what pictures and EVPs we got!! I loved it! It was great.

Beckah: Well, I have to tell you, I was disappointed that I didn't go to the first investigation. However, we did try to go again and, to our immense sadness, the gates were locked and there was no alternative access. The cemetery looked very dark and creepy even during the day. We hope we will eventually be able to get back and investigate further.

Katie: Why am I always the last to know!?

A House In Manchester

"I don't know what to do anymore."
—Client

A woman called us, desperate for anyone to help and understand her situation. Raven listened patiently on the phone as the client went over a list of phenomena. The psychic asked Sharon (the homeowner) to hold on to it till we got there, when we could have a formal interview. So two days later, off we went on a chilly late October night—we bravely ventured forth into an unknown situation…again.

Raven and Lucy, a guest of Ghost Quest, arrived with a bit of apprehension; Raven wondered what we were getting ourselves into and Lucy was excited to be part of the journey. Sharon, the homeowner, and Raven sat down to talk about the background of the home. She told us that there had been activity since they moved in but it had been worsening. Vases and other objects were flying from the walls, there were voices heard, images of a dark man with a grotesque face, and a child was being seen by both adults and children of the house.

As Raven and Sharon talked, it became more apparent to believe that the homeowner herself had abilities. Raven did not bring this to anyone's attention though as she was not one hundred percent certain. As Lucy listened in, she became more excited about the investigation. After the twenty-minute discussion, Sharon led us around the house.

We decided to start upstairs and work our way down. The upstairs held two bedrooms, and in one, Raven made contact with the little girl that the family had been seeing. The child spirit was frightened and would not speak to Raven, so we continued on, determined to help the girl before we left. We checked the second bedroom upstairs and found nothing of interest; we descended the stairs to the first floor where Raven felt drawn to the master bedroom. When we entered, it was like hitting a brick wall of heat and heaviness, we only took a couple steps in and felt an ominous presence that did not want us there. So we humored it and left the room as quickly as possible. Again we talked to Sharon.

Raven needed more insight as to what was happening within the home. She felt that, although the presence did not want us in the room, that did not mean it was negative. Raven came back to her conclusion about Sharon's abilities and began wondering whether the spirit might in fact be connected to the homeowner.

Raven began to ask Sharon more in depth questions about the male presence; the client began to unknowingly tap into the male spirit confirming Raven's belief that there was indeed an attachment. As the spirit opened up to Sharon, she began to grow very hot. She mentioned this to Raven who knew spirits sometimes communicated with psychics by giving them the pains of their death. The medium watched Sharon carefully but not interfering, knowing this was something the woman had to experience.

As Sharon continued to talk, she began to feel lightheaded and dizzy; then to Raven's surprise Sharon said, "Why is everything turning black?" Sharon passed out for a heart-pounding ten seconds. Raven, Lucy, and Sharon's husband, Bill, who had been relatively passive during the investigation, circled the woman's unconscious body. When Sharon's eyes opened, everyone breathed a sigh of relief.

This experience was not all for naught, though, as it opened up communications between the spirit and Raven. The spirit's name was Samuel and he began to tell us a story of racism, rape, and murder.

He lived on the East side of Manchester in the late 1800s with his mother, his father, and his younger sister, who was about twelve years old. Where the client's house stands was once a park, which was close to his home. He went out walking one evening. As he was strolling, he came upon a group of four youths. When they saw him, they attacked and tied a rope around his hands and legs to prevent him from moving.

Unfortunately, although Samuel yelled, it was late at night, and no one heard him. They tortured him by cutting off his hands. As they watched him bleed, they dowsed him in oil, and then set him aflame. Samuel's younger sister had always idolized him, and that night she had followed him on his walk. When she saw what was happening, she bravely stepped forward and tried to defend her older brother. The young men held her captive while she watched her brother die. They then raped her repeatedly as punishment for trying to interfere. After they got their pleasure, they ended her life by slitting her throat and burning her body.

Neither Samuel or his sister knows what happened with the bones and ashes; they were never found. For a time, rumor circulated that the pair had run away, and a formal investigation never took place.

Samuel was stuck in a place of immense anguish; he was angry that no one was listening and did not understand why people reacted to him the way they did. When he appeared to the family, he showed himself as he looked when he had passed, this scared both the homeowners and the children. His anger resulted in the poltergeist activity within the home. Samuel was in such a place that he was not even aware his sister was in the home with him. He was so consumed with getting someone to listen, fearing for his sister and where she might be fueled his resentment toward the living.

After hearing Samuel's story and connecting the two spirits, Sharon felt a lot better, but also grieved for what the pair went through in life and death. We all did. Looking back, Sharon finally got the connection between the events within the home and Samuel's story, now aware of what he had been trying to tell the family since they took residence within the home.

When Raven asked Samuel what he would like to do, he insisted his story be told to others. She promised she would do as he asked. He also wanted to see his parents and sister. Raven contacted her own father who had been deceased for sometime and acted as a helper spirit for her. He connected Samuel to his sister, and Raven's last vision of them was her father's arm on either siblings' shoulder and walking them into the spirit realm so they could finally rest at peace and be reunited with their family.

A House In Manchester Revisited

"Look at that!"

—Raven

It was a cold and drizzly winter night when the Ghost Quest crew was asked to come back to Sharon's home. When we arrived, we noticed there were renovations going on—this can sometimes drum up dormant spirit activity. We also knew Sharon was sensitive to spirits, so they could be trying to communicate. Either way, they were excited to be investigating the house.

As we sat down with Sharon, she described activity reminiscent of Samuel, although Raven and Beckah quickly established he was not here even in visitation. She relayed exactly what was happening. Doors opened by themselves, toys in the children's room were turning on and off or showed signs of being played with, people were being pushed or touched.

There were also a few incidents surrounding the outside work on the house. First, Bill, Sharon's husband, could feel pressure on him and could not continue working. The pressure subsided when he came down from the ladder. Next, a friend of the family was literally pushed off the ladder falling to the hard earth below. Sharon and Bill had decided to put the construction off for a while, until someone could come in to find out what was going on. With the interview finished, we split into two teams with Beckah and Fred heading upstairs and Raven and a guest investigator, Martha, working on the main floor.

Beckah and Fred were both drawn to an area in the girls' room. There we found a small cubbyhole, about three feet high, cut into a wall; it was empty. Beckah began to tap into a pair of children who frequently played upstairs; they lived at the house back in the fifties. Beckah did not feel pain or a feeling of being lost around them, she felt the spirits were in visitation and attracted to the other children in the home. Fred noticed a hole in the wall and took a picture of it. On his camera, there appeared a child's hand and finger pointing at it. The hand did not show up in other pictures of the hole. Meanwhile, Raven and Martha were downstairs getting the willies.

Raven was in the back kitchen area that led out to the porch. She felt the strong presence of "Joseph," an older man who once owned the property. He didn't mind the intruders, but when the owners began to change his home, his possessiveness became apparent. As Raven was explaining what she was hearing to the homeowner, Martha was taken back when she looked at the wall and saw the shadow of a man sitting in a rocking chair. Immediately, cameras started clicking in a greedy attempt to capture the phenomena. We then began a search for a natural explanation, but could not find one.

When we turned back to the wall, the shadow had disappeared—was it Joseph making his presence known? He was insistent that no work be done in the home and would continue to sabotage their renovation, so ultimately Raven had to clear him. After this was done, we moved into the front of the kitchen and Raven encountered Bill's mother who had passed away quite a few years ago. It was an emotional reunion for Bill, Sharon, and the mother. Now made aware that his mom was around, Bill felt relieved that there was at least one spirit they knew in the house. Martha continued to snap pictures and gather EVP evidence.

Beckah and Fred descended the stairs, rejoined us, and after a brief discussion about the nights events, we went back to headquarters. When we reviewed the evidence, four out of seven of the photographs had the shadow of the rocking chair man in them. Along with them was the child's finger in the hole that Fred had taken a picture of upstairs. We had EVPs of a man praying in French, at the time Raven was clearing; we knew this was Joseph as it was Martha's recorder that picked it up. There were also EVPs upstairs of a child's laughter. All in all, it was a wonderful investigation.

We kept in contact with Sharon, and she has finished renovations in her home (which looks great by the way). There has been no phenomena in the house since our last investigation and clearing.

Authors note: Whenever someone has latent abilities, they have the possibility of attracting spirits to them. These are usually spirits who have a desperate need to talk. Unfortunately, if you do not hear them, they feel they are being ignored and this can upset them. Samuel wanted attention and he knew Sharon could hear him. She just wasn't trying. This, believe it or not, is a frequent occurrence. If you have activity, check with a reputable medium that can help.

Evidence

There was some evidence but nothing solid, that didn't matter to us in this case as much though. We were just happy to help the spirit get back with his family. Sometimes evidence really isn't everything.

Photos:
Orbs
Faces in mirror
Finger coming through a hole in the wall

EVPs:
"What?"
"Hmmm"
Mumbling

Personal Experiences:
The owner received the symptoms of Samuel's death, Raven felt extremely uncomfortable when entering the client's bedroom because of the spirits presence. On the second trip, Beckah heard a bang behind her, which was not, picked up on the tape.

Crew's Afterthoughts

Beckah: A very intense investigation. Although we did not experience a lot for paranormal activity, the children were fun to watch and play with.

Raven: The first part of this investigation was incredibly satisfying. Reassuring Samuel that all would be well and watching him go into the light with my father brought tears to my eyes. It was incredible. The second part was interesting. It wasn't one of my favorite investigations, but it was a good.

Katie: I wasn't there, however, the story of Samuel touched me deeply, and I am horrified by the events that happened to him and his sister. I am extremely happy Raven could help them gain peace.

A Haunting In Green Field

"He's not himself."
—Client

A couple had just moved into a beautiful home, and much like in the last case, renovations were going on all throughout their home. Spirit activity had dramatically increased the more they changed the house. Knock, raps, a man's voice, full-body apparitions and a host of other phenomena were taking place, so much so, that the young pregnant owner and her husband were finding it hard to stay there.

Ghost Quest was called in. We approached the road leading up to the house, Raven began to feel sick to her stomach and knew we were both expected and unwanted. Doug was excited by the notion of exploring this highly haunted property.

The home was a beautiful two-story single-family structure. As Raven and Doug entered, Raven felt like she already knew the house. We talked for a short while about what was happening, all the while Raven kept glancing upstairs. Much like Beckah at the Dearborn building, she felt like she was being led to an upstairs bedroom. Walking in she knew there was a male there and that he felt complete ownership of the property. She looked at Mary, the owner's mother and she exclaimed, "This is 'His' bedroom."

She got more in depth as she paced the room. She felt he was from the 1850s—not necessarily from this particular house but from a structure that was there before the current place was. He was tall with a full head of hair, wore a jacket with a large lapel, and he was angry. She also knew that he was grounded here. She felt a strong connection to him, in fact, she knew he was attaching to her because she could hear him so clearly.

By this time, Doug had made his way into the room, taking pictures on his journey upstairs with his digital camera. When he reached the bedroom door, he took a picture of the owner's mother and Raven standing by a window. In the picture, Raven was so connected to this spirit, and their energy so connected, that it was as though she was channeling, and this caused her to appear transparent in the picture. Everything else was solid. We did try to recreate the phenomena but couldn't. While in the room, the medium attempted to take pictures, but every time she did, the batteries would drain and her camera would instantly die. She tried three or four sets of batteries, but couldn't take a single picture until

Raven connecting with spirit. She has gone transparent.

we finally left the room. Oftentimes, this happens because spirits use the energy contained in batteries for fuel. It helps them to get stronger and create more phenomena.

Raven continued to communicate what she heard from the man. His name was Joseph and he had a wife and two young children when he was among the living. He was still very adamant that this was his house. It was his place and he didn't like people messing about his things. Why did they have to change everything and why all the noise and chatter? He was upset. Not the type to hurt anyone, but angry nonetheless.

The owner relayed how her husband seemed to be isolating himself in a room in the cellar. He became more fixated

Orb in motion and one in the window outside the house.

on the renovations, he no longer wanted anything changed in the home. Finally, when his wife attempted to remove the old light fixture and install the new one, the husband became very irate, showing his connection to the spirits. This was typical for the type of haunting they were experiencing. She also told us as we descended the stairs she had felt touches and heard tapping in the walls at night. It seemed this spirit really wanted to make his presence felt and he was succeeding.

Raven, Doug, and the owners went through the entire house including all the nooks and crannies. What we found were a lot of mundane spirits, some related to the family, others not, but the only active one was this man. Although there were no other incidences beyond those upstairs, we

Orb outside the house.

knew this was a place to come back to. We were also in awe of the amount of orbs that showed up as we took pictures in other parts of the house, and the EVPs were spectacular. The owners did not request a clearing at that time, and when we last heard, all was quiet.

Evidence

There was a lot of EVP evidence, and plenty for photos. Here we are just listing a couple.

Orb leaving the fire pit in the backyard.

Photos:
Orbs outside the house
Orbs inside the house
Man in sliding door

EVPs:
"Get Out"
"Watch the steps"
"Marie"

Personal Experiences:
The client's husband has his own experiences, as did his wife who heard and felt tapping. The crew didn't have any personal experiences.

Living room littered with orbs.

Crew Afterthoughts

Raven: This was a very typical haunting with plenty of evidence in photos. I enjoyed this investigation and felt very good about the outcome.

Beckah: I was not there, but it is a very interesting case and can show how easily it is to be affected by a spirit and not even know. I think this gives a perfect example of spirit possession and manipulation.

Katie: Awesome case, wish I had been there. I thought the photo of Raven invisible was fantastic and I'm happy to know the husband will willingly be continuing the renovations.

Beech Street

"The man is going."

—EVP

On Sunday, January 2, 2005, the Ghost Quest crew stood outside a modest dormitory-style four-story boarding house on Beech Street. The property managers who lived and worked there reported a smell of beer lingering on the third floor near the attic entrance, children running in the attic, and the feeling of being watched and threatened in the basement. Also, they had two pet snakes they kept down in the cellar in a covered tank; someone had let them out. This wouldn't have been a big deal but, the basement is locked and only the managers have the key…odd.

We decided an investigation was definitely in order and started upstairs in the attic. On the way, the smell of beer assaulted our senses; as we continued upstairs, it got worse. The attic was one room, completely bare with wallpaper and paint cracking and peeling from the walls. Obviously, this room was never remodeled or used.

Beckah immediately began to sense two children hiding in a closet; she felt they were siblings and saw them to be between six and eight years old. They were scared of Beckah. They shied away from her and would not speak. She told Raven and Sandy of what she saw. Raven, being a mother herself, had more sway with the two children; they recognized a female authority figure and connected with her. As she talked with them, she found out that their names were Anna and James, that the attic was the bedroom in their old house, and that they lived around 1938. She asked if the two would like to see their parents, and the two kids became ecstatic; so Raven fulfilled her promise and gave the children a wonderful reunion. The parents escorted their offspring to the other side.

We headed back down the attic steps to the third floor, the smell of beer again assaulting us. The third floor was a long corridor with four rooms off either side. Immediately Raven and Beckah were drawn to the first room on the right. We both saw a man sitting on the bed. He had short brown hair with long sideburns and looked to be from the seventies. We felt the beer smell was connected to him. He had lived and died in the building, and was a harmless spirit who just wanted to "chill." The managers decided to let him do just that. However, Raven requested he not emit the horrific smell of stale beer that seemed to be his calling card. He agreed.

We descended the stairs, scanning for spirits as we went. Our tape recorders had been rolling, and pictures were being taken all throughout the investigation so far. The first and second floors seemed fine; then we hit the basement door. Immediately, heaviness descended, typical of spirit activity. The managers showed us the tank where the snakes had escaped; it looked to be a seventy-gallon fish tank with a sunlight and snap-on cover that was tough for even our investigators to remove. We deduced that there was no way the reptiles could have gotten out themselves, and there were no signs of a way out or of the snakes existence in the cellar. They had been missing for more than a year. No one had seen them; there were no smells of rotting, so obviously the snakes were not dead.

As we went to the back of the cellar, Raven saw a man standing almost in waiting. She felt a cruel power emanating off of him. Behind him, however, she saw a large void, a black portal, which Raven felt he used to gain access to the home. Raven knew that if too many people got close, he would attack, and he would be relentless. So instead of charging she calmly walked forward toward him, the first words out of her mouth were, "I am not afraid of you." She called to the angels, to her ancestors, to rid the home of the spirit. She advised that we stay at a distance and await her word to open the basement door and then the back door.

As the entities she called in struggled with the spirit, Beckah watched in amazement, never having seen her colleague call in such beings. The battle continued for fifteen to twenty minutes, each side gaining and losing their edge.

Then, suddenly, Raven gave the cue to open the doors, and Beckah ran to get the basement door open and then the back door. Immediately, everyone noticed a difference in the basement; the air was not so heavy and a peace descended upon the building.

When we reviewed the evidence, we got a couple of orbs in the pictures—nothing to really blow us away. The EVPs, on the other hand, were pretty amazing. When Beckah, who always wore a backwards baseball cap, oversized jeans, and shirt ascended the stairs, you hear the two children whisper, "Who's the man?" and then as she leaves during the investigation to go to the bathroom, you hear the children say, "The man is going." We didn't get EVPs from the man on the third floor, but the basement was unbelievable! As soon as we descend to the basement it sounded as if you were in a hurricane that breathed. Raven, who had a recorder with her, could not be heard for about fifteen minutes then you hear her shout, "OPEN THE DOOR!" Then the sound of the hurricane-like winds dissipates and all returns to a normal environment.

When contacted for follow-up interviews, both managers stated that the tenants were no longer argumentative and they had moved their gym equipment down to the cellar—that was how comfortable they had become within the building. We are happy we could help and wish them the best.

Evidence

There was nothing really for photos but the EVPs shined. Although there were only three, they were some of the clearest EVPs, we had ever gotten.

Photos:
One photo with two orbs in attic room

EVPs:
"The man is going."
"I don't want to."
Roaring down in basement till clearing is over.

Personal Experiences:
Raven felt heaviness, like walking through snow, felt the illness the children in the attic died from, and felt sensations of a heart attack when she first made contact with the male beer-drinking spirit. Beckah saw her first physical spirit, and everyone smelled the beer.

Crew Afterthoughts

Raven: This was one of the most hair-raising clearings I have done, not because of what happened during the clearing, but because of what was on the tape. The clearing itself was intense and powerful, but hearing such a negative spirit really just blew my mind!

Beckah: Beech Street was very intense. I've never seen Raven work with the entities she used that day. The only thing that bothered me, was that the children thought I was a man.

Katie: I wasn't there, but I wish I could have been! I think from reading the case file that Raven did a terrific job holding her own in an unknown negative environment.

An Infested Apartment

"I Know Where God Comes From. He Comes From Dust."

—Jenna

Katie was called in to investigate a possible demonic haunting. She asked Beckah to assist because she had a feeling there was more there than just inhuman spirits. The client's sister had contacted the demonologist, looking for understanding and some answers. Jenna, the client, had a spirit in her home about twenty-four years ago. She and her sister had used a Ouija board she told us, "I didn't open the Ouija board to have fun; there were spirits in my house and I wanted to know who they were."

We could understand that, but also knew a lot of cases started out that way. She went on to explain that during the first session, spirits did come through. The entities asked the sisters a lot of questions but the girls did not get a lot for answers.

Intrigued, Jenna decided to use the board again— this time alone. She made contact with entities; they said they had been looking for her, that they loved her. They told her, "We're here because God wants us here." She believed them; they were kind and she explained, "They were more honest with me then God was; at least I was getting answers from them."

She grew more and more obsessed, activity increased within her home, and she would wake up in the middle of the night paralyzed, unable to breath or speak. Walls would shake, religious pictures would fly off the walls, water would turn on and off by itself. Usually, right after playing the board. It got to the point where she would have her children stay up at night and watch her sleep because she was so afraid. She also confided, "They said my mother was with them." Her mother had recently passed and so she felt she had to go through the spirits in order to talk to her mother. She would smell feces and feel sick whenever she played with the board, but still was convinced the entities were there for the best.

Twenty-four years later, after several moves and years of pain caused by the entities around her, she now asks, "Where's God in all this; why is He doing this to me?" Religious pictures, crosses, and statuettes litter her apartment. She is a devout Christian and told us," I love my God so much that on Mother's Day and Father's Day, I make them a card and thank them for creating me."

Her apartment is dim, and although it has large open windows and a French sliding door, the air was stale and smelled faintly of trash, though it was spotless. She told us, "I can see Satan; they told me on the board they had to come through Satan to find me. So now I can see him and I tell him to kiss my butt everyday." Although it is the opinion of both investigators that she does not, in fact, see Satan himself, we do believe she is seeing an inhuman spirit that is around her.

We couldn't blame Jenna for having a negative attitude with all that she had been through. She summed up her feelings saying,"I feel forgotten, unloved, used and abused; no one cares." We reminded her that God did love her, but he had no control over free will. By using the Ouija board she freely invited these entities into her home.

Jenna likes to draw and offered to show us a few of her pictures, we agreed thinking this might give us some insight as to what she sees in her daily life. The images were both shocking and interesting. A cross she had created was almost identical to one that Katie used as part of an occult seal for protection. She drew spirits she was seeing and had names for them all.

Anthony was a foreigner and wore a while robe. There was Mary, who was killed; she had lived in San Francisco. Jenna said, "She is a b---- and causes me to do things I don't want to do." For instance, Mary had taken over once, went out, and slashed someone's tires within the building. When Jenna came back to awareness, she was standing next to the car with a nail file in her hand and cried to God, "What did

I do God, why do you let these things happen?!"

It is shown that often people attacked by demonic phen-emena either invite it by messing with the occult or they are people of faith. Jenna was both. She claimed that although she was constantly around negative entities, she was closer to God than ever! She had seen visions of Mother Mary all in white with a rosary, telling her she would be okay. She talked to God daily and felt his presence at some of her worst mo-ments.

An often seen, occurrence with demonic haunting is the manifestation of sudden psychic ability within one of the residents. Jenna displayed such when talking to her sister a week before. Jenna warned Karen saying,"Whatever you do, don't let them come." Karen who had come to be with us during the meeting with Jenna did not know until that moment what her sister meant.

Katie is a gifted demonologist with the ability to see the inhuman and the occult knowledge and to cast them from a home or person. She thought about the woman's situation as she walked the rooms, recognizing it as the third stage of possession, aptly named the Stage of Oppression. This is when the inhuman entities invite their friends to an open house, where the victim is completely under their thumbs. During Katie's walk-through, she noticed not only full-grown demons, but also young offspring, as well as finding a closet filled with babies. The only obvious conclusion was that the inhuman spirits had been breeding here for a long time.

Katie recognized that although there were quite a few inhuman entities, there were not any upper-level demons; they seemed to be low-level demonic and would be quite easy to get rid of. Beckah, on the other hand, had more of an issue helping the spirits cross. It seems that with the demonic came some psychic ability; this in turn

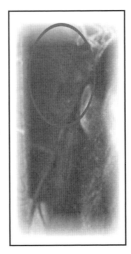

A demonic entity screams in Jesus' ear.

opened Jenna up to seeing and hearing spirits herself. There were six spirits that she became attached to over the years, growing accustomed to them and even forming a friendship. In a contradictory fashion, she explained that she did not want them to go, but did not want them to stay here, as they kept her awake wanting to talk or hearing them cry.

So, Beckah began the process of clearing. She asked Jenna to call her spirits to her. First Steve came to her; he was a man from the fifties and he had told her his story repeatedly. He was a man who had abused his wife, and was lost in his own anger and regret. He found a likeness of pain and suffering in Jenna, and attached to her, they shared their stories and connected, forming a friendship, which the reclusive woman had never truly had before. Jenna wanted to give Stephen relief.

So Beckah began to show Stephen the way home. The spirit was afraid to go, afraid of judgment, and punishment for his actions Beckah knew the only way to get him to go was to bring in the abuser's wife. Chantel came quickly, offering forgiveness to her husband. He wept, and kept apologizing for his drunkenness, his anger, and his horrific punishment. His wife brought him to the light, although he told Jenna, "If you ever needed me, I would come back."

So it proceeded for the next two hours, misguided spirit after misguided spirit was connected with a loved one and brought to the light, each promising to return if needed.

Katie began to use her aspergillum, chanting sacred texts, cornering inhuman entities and creating seals to destroy them. She cleansed the breeding closet, where most of the babies were kept. After another hour and a half, she had finally cleansed the house of the demons.

All in all we had helped twenty separate spirits to the other side, eight full-grown demons and twenty-seven off-spring. Finally we became aware of a cat! Jenna explained that the cat had always been nervous within the home, and never came out from his hiding place. Well today he did and he wanted to talk!

During the interview with Jenna she gave us insight into her current belief stating, "I know where God comes from. He comes from dust." At the same time that she says this, trumpets can be heard playing a peaceful lulling melody, although no music was heard within the home itself. Also there is a multitude of demonic chatter throughout the tape, and we noticed throughout the tape that the victim's voice took on subtle changes of tone and sound of voice.

Katie had taken a photo of a picture of Jesus the client had in her bedroom. In it, you can see a demonic entity screaming in his ear. This is typical of inhuman spirits. Demons will mock anything religious, crosses, Jesus—they aren't picky. Also we got spirits within the mirrors at the home, including Steve.

Two months later, we received a phone call from Karen; she was distraught and upset with her sister. It seems that Jenna could not become used to living alone and had invited all of the spirits back to her side. Now she could not get rid of them. When we contacted Jenna, she refused our help and denied knowledge of spirits within her home. We felt this was her way of "protecting" them.

Not long after that she called Raven and asked her to come in and clear. After a half hour's discussion Raven came to the conclusion that the woman did not really want help.

Evidence

There was a lot of evidence for this case, very weird evidence.

Photos:
Demon screaming in Jesus' ear
Spirit leaning away from flash in kitchen mirror
Demonic entity in hallway mirror
Mists surrounding victim
Orbs around Beckah
Ectoplasm in bathroom

EVPs:
Client talking about praying then, "Jesus! Jesus! Jesus!"
Demonic clicking, and chatter through out tape.
Sounds like you're in a hurricane till after clearing.

"Sssshh," said while Katie was telling client of difference between human and inhuman spirits.

Trumpets play a beautiful melody when client says, "I know where God comes from. He comes from dust."

Personal Experiences:
Beckah felt creeped all throughout the investigation; Katie was pushed when she went in the bedroom, Jenna's sister got extreme headaches when she talked about religion.

Crew's After Thoughts

Raven: Although I wasn't there to participate in this investigation, I did review some of the evidence. Katie and Beckah did a phenomenal job in an environment that was intensely negative and stressful. This only serves to prove how valuable and needed a demonologist is and our Katie is one of the best!

Beckah: You know I really have to say I'm sorry for the woman, I feel that I helped her to the best of my ability, and I am proud of the job I did. After living with the spirits for that long, I am not surprised she called them back; it must have been lonely not having the company she was used to occupying the home. I have the utmost appreciation for Jenna, opening up her home and spirits to us and I wish her all the best.

Katie: I think this is a perfect example for those who play with psychic boards or tamper with the occult, without experience or training. It was a very intense and tiresome case; the infestation was extreme and I don't think I've ever seen such a concentration of demonic energy in such a small space.

Stark Cemetery

"I believe in the resurrection of the dead."
—Grave Inscription

On a whim Katie and Beckah drove through rural New Hampshire. It was a cool and crisp fall day, with clear blue skies, a perfect time for an afternoon drive. We came across a picturesque gravesite called Stark Cemetery. A wall encompassed the street entrance with a small iron gate in the center. At first look, we were upset thinking we wouldn't be able to check it out. Then Katie, determined to find a way in, noticed a set of three small stairs that were built into the wall; it was the same on the other side, another set of three let us into a small clearing.

Since it was autumn, leaves littered the ground, crunching beneath our feet. Beckah felt an inviting energy as we approached the iron gated enclosure that held the headstones. Again we looked for an entrance and found another stone wall piece with three stairs. Katie began taking pictures, remembering we had an open Ghost Quest this night; we decided to recommend the spot and drove straight to the headquarters.

When we told Raven of the quaint little cemetery we found, she agreed it might be fun to check out. We took along a guest—her name was Jackie; she had been on previous Ghost Quest cases and was a joy to have accompany us on this one. When Beckah told everyone of the inviting energy, we began to expect the night to be equally peaceful, and a very nice break from some of the more hazardous cases we had been having recently.

We arrived at dusk; Beckah and Katie showed the other crew members how to get over the wall. As Raven descended the stairs, she felt a wall of energy hit her. She commented on it saying, "It's not negative, just old." As we all walked towards the cemetery, Beckah noted that there were about six visible headstones outside the iron enclosure, separating it from the rest. Jackie thought maybe it had been a previous family plot and they just didn't see the need to move the graves. Beckah shrugged and hopped over the steps and into the cemetery. Although the rest of the night she had made up her mind to go and check out the other headstones before she left.

As darkness fell upon our investigation, we turned on our flashlights and continued to take pictures, call out to spirits to make noise, show themselves in our photos, or speak on our tapes. Katie who was determined to get some sort of spirit activity, threatened that we would leave if no one was going to show him or herself. We believe the threat worked

View from entrance of Stark Cemetery.

because the next picture Katie took, of a beautiful celtic cross headstone, there was an orb flying away from it, and quickly she took another and caught it leaving her frame!

We began to get more excited, feeling as though we finally had the spirits attention. Jackie, who is sensitive, picked up on spirit energy by a large statue of Jesus that seemed to be protecting the gravesite, and Raven picked up on a woman named Elizabeth, who she felt came from the early Victorian era. She described the spirit as a statuesque woman with curly brown hair put in an ornate *updo* with a lacey dress that buttoned to her neck. She told Raven, "I died, I went with my family, I come back once in a while and make sure everything is tidy."

To which Raven asked, "Are you in this cemetery?"

Elizabeth then rolled her eyes and told the medium, "No, no, my family is."

Raven asked which grave was a relative and Elizabeth pointed to an ornate headstone with what looked like a military insignia. When Raven turned around to ask another question, it seemed the spirit had seen fit to go and check other headstones at other cemeteries. We smiled as we continued our investigation, intrigued by Elizabeth's spirit and sarcasm. As she had said, we did not find her tombstone there, however it did jog Beckah's memory about the other stones lying outside the enclosure.

The surrounding area was pitch black, but she bravely made her way over the steps. Seeing Beckah on the other side of the gate, Jackie joined her, flashlight in hand, for which Beckah was relieved. Upon arriving at the first row of three headstones, the name Belinda caught Beckah's eye, the tablet marked three names in all: Samuel, Belinda, and another name neither Beckah or Jackie could figure out.

Although she felt no presences in this area, Beckah began to call out for Samuel or Belinda in a feeble attempt to gain contact from either of the two spirits. As she sat in front of their grave, she noticed an inscription; Beckah always believed grave inscriptions told a lot about the dead and their family. This particular saying was simple and eerie. It said, "I believe in the resurrection of the dead." She looked up at Jackie, repeating the inscription, Beckah's crewmate simply said, "Oh my goodness." We decided to head back inside the cemeteries small iron gates, but on the walk we both noticed it was dramatically colder outside them then inside. Beckah accounted this to the energies that permeated inside the cemetery.

We checked our watches and realized it was a quarter to eleven, time to head back and review evidence. On our drive back, Beckah and Jackie recounted the grave inscription and difference in temperatures. Raven agreed with the theory Beckah had come up with regarding the differences in energy intensity and heat. That settled, the crew relaxed and enjoyed the rest of the quiet ride.

When we arrived back at Ghost Quest Headquarters, we looked over our evidence. The only piece we really had was Katie's pictures of the two orbs; there were some murmurings, but we discounted it as it was when Beckah and Jackie were separated from the rest of the group and it could have been them talking. All in all, it was a fun and relaxing night.

Evidence

There were a couple of exciting points during this investigation such as the differences in temperature and the ominous headstone inscription. Unfortunately there was not much for evidence.

Photos:
Celtic cross headstone, Orb
Another headstone, Orb
Orb next to Beckah
Small mist next to Jackie

EVPs:
None

Personal Experiences:
There were no other personal experiences felt during this case.

Inscription on a grave, "I believe in the resurrection of the dead."

Historical Facts about Stark Cemetery
  ❖ In 1962, the graves were moved from Winslow Road to Stark Road because of the Hopkinton Everrett Flood Control Project; they were afraid that the cemetery was below flood line.
  ❖ A grave on the outside of the cemetery is inscribed with, "I believe in the resurrection of the dead."
  ❖ Dunbarton Historical Society leased the cemetery site and had it dedicated as Stark Memorial Park in 1971 and continues to maintain it.
  ❖ There are five graves with Unknown bodies they are shown as Unknown 1, Unknown 2 and so on.

Crew Afterthoughts

Raven: It was a good investigation, very interesting; getting in touch with Elizabeth was a very neat experience. She was a nice lady.

Beckah: I thought it was a wonderful little site. I especially loved the gravestone with the engraving "I believe in the resurrection of the dead." It was such a powerful message and the heat anomaly was fascinating.

Katie: I thought this was a delightful little find. I don't feel there was a lot of activity, but it was a nice break from the really active cases we had been having lately.

Raven's Shop

In 2003, Raven and two friends decided to open a store. Beckah, who was very close to Raven, wanted to come onboard and Raven was overjoyed at the prospect of having her. The structure was 2,200 square feet including a back room with a large front selling space, a docking bay, cellar, and office for readings. The only problem we soon discovered was the spirits in it.

At the shop preparing for Halloween. Guess we weren't the only ones!

Our issues started from the beginning, as we renovated, put up shelving and so on; our tools would move. Every time we put up a shelf, it would come down, although the screws stayed in the wall and were firm.

Our motion sensor alarm system would go off at night for no reason, and it was always the door to the entrance of the docking bay. When you walked in there, you always felt as though you were being watched—you just knew you weren't alone. There was a lot of tension among the management and it seemed the more resentment and anger that was tossed around, the more the spirits got active.

By second day, we had one co-worker leave and another left three months later. The tension had released. Now we had time to get down to the real business.

Day-to-day life went smoothly. There were still paranormal phenomena around the shop, but we took it in stride. The spirits wanted us to know they were there, and we accepted that. A female spirit often showed herself in the office window; the cash register would open itself, products would be moved or turned, banging in the docking bay, and steps coming up the stairs from the basement (the entrance of which was in the docking bay). That was fine though, till the day of the robbery.

We opened up shop that morning, half awake, with coffee in hand. As we made our way to the back room, we passed the counter. Beckah did a double take, then tapped Raven on the shoulder saying, "Hey, where is the cash register and where is my axe?" We looked around the other side of the counter and there was the cash register beaten up on the floor with the axe we always had hung on the wall next to it.

We both chuckled because all together there was maybe two dollars in change. We went to the back room to call the police, then we noticed a large handprint on one of the windows, the screen was torn beyond repair, and the refrigerator was open.

As Raven called the police, Beckah went around to make sure nothing else was missing. That's when she noticed the large hole next to the docking bay door. She opened the door all the way—it was not light being made of solid wood. The hole was caused by the top corner of the door which had a door stopper. With that established, she walked into the docking bay. The door there stood wide open. Obviously the criminal got scared, but by what?

The security alarm was a silent one, set off by door triggers and motion sensor; why didn't it go off? There were so many questions. We had to get answers and we knew there were witnesses in the building. The spirits.

The police came, got our reports, and took fingerprints from the window. Beckah and Raven showed them the door hole and they agreed something had definitely scared him off, but even they couldn't tell us what. We decided to conduct our own investigation. We took out the spirit board and began asking questions. Immediately a woman name Rosa Lee came forward telling us last night's tale. Here is what she told us:

A man of five feet eight inches, late forties, came in, with a friend. She said we had seen this man before, but we didn't know him. Rosa Lee told us he looked like a "common laborer" and he came through the backroom. She said he was cold; he kept rubbing his hands together. First he went to the cash register. He threw it down on the floor hoping it would break. When the lock didn't loosen, he attacked it with the axe. He kept trying to break the lock. He finally gave up and went to the refrigerator to see if we had anything good to eat. Rosa Lee said she didn't like the noise or the mess and that she wouldn't stand for it and she told him so. When he felt her presence, he ran, thinking someone had come in. He threw open the docking bay door and left the premises.

Now we couldn't confirm anything she had said because we didn't have cameras, but the next day, we had a young woman visit the shop asking if we had been robbed. When Beckah answered in the affirmative, she claimed she had been too. She had employed a plow man, who as it turned out had also stopped at our shop a couple times looking to add us to his clientele. Funny enough, he was in his mid-forties, he was around five feet eight inches, and he was a common laborer, with ripped carpenter's jeans and a shirt with paint all over it. He told us he used to do handyman and plow work for the previous storeowners. The woman told us he got about $150 from her, and we told her he probably got about twenty-two cents from us.

After she left, we sent up silent thanks to Rosa Lee. We now believe she decided to scare off our thief. The information she gave us was too specific to not have been true.

Since we had made communication with our resident spirit, she made herself more known, she grew bolder in her appearances. Beckah would often see her walking up the steps from the basement, and when she would stock shelves, items would turn and straighten on their own. It looked as though we did have a third manager, and the best thing was, we didn't have to pay her!

Through the next few months we met Sandy, Ben, Doug, Katie, and Fred. Together we formed Ghost Quest and we used the shop as our home base. Conducting investigations at night and working during the day wore down some of Beckah and Raven's defenses and a couple of times we took entities back to the shop with us.

A couple of days after a Ghost Quest, Raven asked Beckah if she would take Rayna, Raven's youngest daughter to the dentist while Raven minded the store. Beckah agreed and Raven was left alone to handle customers. It was a slow afternoon and Raven went into the back and began working on the books for the shop.

As she began calculating expenditures, she heard a dog growl. Thinking maybe one was outside, she looked out the windows in the back, then the front—no dogs. This made her a little nervous, but she sat back down and continued her work. A few moments later she heard it again, this time sounding like it was three feet from her. Raven shook it off, but was beginning to feel apprehensive when it happened again, much louder!

Raven quickly signed off from the computer, shut off all the lights, and went to the dental office shaking as she was driving. "It's okay to hear or see a ghost, but a growling dog?!" Raven thought as her head spun. When she located Beckah, she began to relax, and through talking to her colleague, realized she probably wouldn't hear from the dog again.

All things being good, we headed in bright and early the next morning. No dog and no growls. Raven was a happy camper. Later on that evening, Sandy and Ben came by the shop. We were all sitting in the back talking. Raven, behind her desk, had a perfect view of two of the four back windows.

Raven turned to Beckah and pointed at the window, she couldn't believe her eyes. Taking up the entire two part glass of the large window was a man's face. He had the look of someone from the eighteenth century. A top hat graced his head, large circular black glasses, kind eyes, handle-bar moustache and an oval face was peering over at the opposite corner of the room. Beckah looked at Raven as she sat there with her mouth on the floor. "Beckah, look at the window!"

The minute Raven spoke these words; the face turned and stared at her. She wasn't scared, but after the last instance with the dog, Raven was a little nervous. Beckah turned her face away and said, "I'm not looking," as she walked over and drew down the shade.

Ghost Quest decided to do an investigation. We set up our equipment, and it wasn't long before we began to gather evidence. Orbs, pictures of mists, EVPs—they had everything. This is the information Beckah and Raven received.

Rosa Lee, it seems, was a resident in one of the upstairs apartments, but not only that, she was more like a caretaker. She died of natural causes. The dog, Beckah felt, was brought back from an investigation; the man in the top hat was just passing by. We cleared the shop of the dog and the man, but left Rosa Lee in peace. Oh, the joys of being at the shop. Think this was the end? It wasn't!

On a sunny day, a young woman came into the shop with her husband. He threw off a lot of negative energy, and although Raven and Beckah were being polite, he left in a bit of a huff.

He showed up later at a party we hosted. Everything was going well and we had been having a wonderful time until he began to complain about the energy in the room and stormed out. Both Beckah and Raven dismissed it as his probably having a bad day and continued on with the party. By the end of the week following this event, customers had almost completely stopped coming to the shop.

Beckah and Raven began to get nervous, as not only the shop seemed to be affected by these troubled times we were having. Disputes began with both of us and Rayna. (Raven's youngest daughter was also affected.) One night after closing, we had gathered at the shop. After a month of no business and things getting steadily worse, we both needed to vent. None of us could believe what we were hearing and wanted to take some kind of action to find out what we were dealing with. We set up an investigation.

EVPs were caught, but nothing conclusive. Katie, unsure of what was causing the disturbances, called upon her knowledge and gifted Beckah and Raven with a special old occult recipe to prevent negative energy from coming into the shop. After this was done Beckah said, "That's it; let's check out the talking board and see what we can find out."

We all gathered in the psychic room to try and contact the spirit (or spirits) that were affecting the shop. The board began to spell out gibberish, and just as we were about to stop, a name came through—Oscar. It seems Oscar was a spirit who liked to cause problems. He took what had begun soon after the couples visit and combined it with some of the negative residual energy of both the shop and its owners, making things worsen exponentially.

Everyone breathed a sigh of relief. We had a reason and a name. Beckah and Katie led the clearing. This time it would be a powerful one to rid the shop, the people, and any residual negativity from the shop. The most wondrous thing was that after the clearing was over, everyone began to smile, joke, and laugh. It had truly taken. Everything was back to normal. There were no outstanding ghostly experiences in the shop after that, well that is until we closed our doors.

Although closing the door was necessary, it was emotional too, this had been our place for over a year. We had gone to hell and back here, found friends, love, and ourselves. But we also had connected with a couple of the spirits there, specifically Rosa Lee. She became an active participant in our shop life. Most of our clients knew about her and would greet her as they came in.

We were almost done moving, and Amanda and Raven had rented a van so we could move some of the displays.

While they were out, Beckah was at the shop alone. She was moving everything she could into the docking bay, holding the door open with a chair. After moving a hutch, she went into the backroom to sit for a moment. As she sat drinking her water and nursing her aching back, the door in the docking bay slammed shut. Beckah jumped up and ran to the door thinking maybe someone had come in. The chair was two feet away from the door. Someone had moved it, but was it human or spirit?

As Beckah investigated the chair, she came to the conclusion that there was no way the chair would have moved itself. The back docking bay and front doors were locked, so she knew it wasn't human. A little nervously she called out to Rosa Lee, telling her to stop it, explaining that we had to leave. In the backroom there was still a desk, worktable, chairs, and another hutch. Beckah began sweeping the front room, needing to work, otherwise she would run. As she swept she heard footsteps behind her, but no one was there.

Just keep sweeping, she thought. *They can't hurt you.* But she knew they could make her feel terrified, that they were upset, and would make her feel very, very uncomfortable. Then she heard a scraping sound in the backroom. Already a little panicky she meekly looked into the room—everything was moved. It was as if someone had a hissy fit. Papers were strewn across the floor, and chairs were knocked over. Beckah called Raven, "I can't take it anymore Raven, this is just too much; they are all over and wicked active."

Immediately Raven knew whom she was talking about. "Wait outside in the driveway hun. They can't hurt you; you'll be okay. Just tell them to stop."

"I did already; they won't; they've gone nuts! I don't feel like it's all Rosa Lee though," Beckah said as she made her way out to the driveway behind the store.

"Tap into it then," Raven recommended.

Beckah nervously attempted to do just that while still on the phone. "This is a guy. I've seen him a couple of times before. He was here during the fire. I don't know why he is angry with us, but he is." As she said this, the docking bay door slammed shut. "Oh crap, oh crap; Raven, you need to get back NOW!"

"I'm on my way; just hang tight." Raven and Amanda drove as quickly as they could back to Beckah, fearing for their friend.

When we arrived back at the shop, it was to find a completely distraught and agitated Beckah. She paced the driveway hugging herself. Raven got out of the van and hugged Beckah, then asked for the complete story. As Beckah recounted everything, Amanda went into the shop to investigate, she saw the mess the shop was in and knew something was just not right. Instead of clearing the spirit, we moved all of our stuff on the last van run, and did not look back. Although we all swear, to this day that when we drove away, there was someone looking out the window.

Evidence

The shop had a lot of evidence; listed below.

Photos:
Orbs in the back room
Many orbs on the dock bay
Apparition reflected in the front window

EVPs:
"Hey Man"
"Don't go"
Growl of a dog

Personal Experiences:
Many people, Beckah, Raven, and visitors of the shop felt touches while there. Raven and Beckah both used to feel like they were followed, especially coming in the docking bay.

Crew Afterthoughts

Raven: The time at the shop was both wonderful and, at times, hair-raising. I often wonder if people there now have any issues. I know we did! Now that years have passed I would love to go back and re-investigate the property.

Beckah: Working at the shop was an experience itself. Cohabitating with the spirits there was both scary and enlightening. I think they wanted me to leave just about as much as I wanted to go. I miss the shop and the spirits in it. I would love to go back and just investigate!

Katie: Being in the shop was a blast, the people there were great and so were the spirits. I spent a lot of money there! The spirits were really active and it made for an amazing experience.

University of New Haven

Though a New Hampshire group, Ghost Quest also serves locales surrounding their primary area in New England. The following case, though outside New Hampshire, was a great case for the group.

Raven, representing Ghost Quest was invited to Connecticut by Professor Al Bradshaw, to conduct a lecture on death and suicide for a class of college students at University of New Haven and Southern Connecticut University. Raven, along with a guest, Denise McMahon, traveled there not realizing we were going to be part of not one, but two awesome Ghost Quests. Professor Bradshaw, his wife, and many wonderful students went along as investigators during the two investigations.

The first part took place on the top floor of Maxie Hall. At one time it was an orphanage and now houses offices and classrooms. We walked up the stairs to Maxie and the expectations were palpable. Students had heard stories about this place for years and shared some of those stories with us. We felt that we were finally going to get the answer to the question: Was it haunted? As students gathered on both sides of the most haunted wing of Maxie Hall, Raven began to call out to spirits. Cameras flashed and orbs were caught, both with the camera and with the naked eye, and everyone was so excited. The rush heightened as movement was caught underneath the door at the end of the corridor. A black shape moved slowly back and forth in the empty room. The students were in awe; so was Raven. After spending about an hour talking, taking pictures, and gathering EVPs, they retired for the evening.

Back at our hotel room, both Raven and Denise heard banging on the wall. This wall was an outside wall on the seventh floor. There was no evidence gathered at this time, but it served to keep them on edge for the next days activities.

The next evening, we all gathered to investigate a large cemetery in the middle of New Haven. This cemetery had a long history of paranormal activity, or so the students had told Raven. The cemetery was meticulously cared for and extended about a half mile from one end to the other. We pulled into a cul-de-sac and got out. We gathered together and began to walk through the cemetery, Professor Bradshaw and the students eagerly chattering behind us.

Raven pointed out how to feel energy from the headstones, which shocked a lot of the people, including Professor Bradshaw, as we felt heat emitted from some of these stones. She also drew them to where she was feeling activity. The camera began to click, and one fellow took a picture with a huge orb by a tree. Raven told Denise, "I don't think I have ever seen someone get quite that excited about an orb. Good one though," and she smiled.

Further into the cemetery, Raven encountered a new first, for her. All eyes looked to where Raven was pointing. This was the very first time Raven and most of the group had seen orbs of all colors literally bouncing off headstones. She had seen a random orb before, but never so many moving so much. Cameras were clicking like mad in an effort to get proof of what they were seeing.

Moving further into the cemetery, some of the students recounted the tale of "Midnight Mary." She was a young girl, who according to legend, passed from illness and was buried alive in the cemetery. Someone heard her screaming, but when her grave was finally opened, it was too late. Mary had tried to scratch her way through her coffin. Her nails were gone and there was blood everywhere. Her hair was stuck to her head with sweat from the effort it took. She was a disturbing child of pain and torment. Her legendary tomb validates this.

This is the legend: It is also said that she makes herself apparent to those who are in the cemetery at midnight. The inscription, and this is paraphrased, says that if you linger by her gravesite at midnight, you would not survive the night. We were slowly drawn to her gravesite, and sure enough, on the stone itself the legend was written.

Although nothing was audibly heard while we were there, we did get a magnificent orb over her stone just as the group gathered there. Was Midnight Mary watching us? We think so.

All in all, this was an extremely interesting and fun investigation and one we definitely need to go back to.

Evidence

Although there wasn't much for hard evidence, this case gave us all new experiences!

Photos:
Orb over grave
Orbs jumping from headstone to headstone

EVPs:
Nothing for evidence

Personal Experiences:
Orbs were physically seen

History of New Haven
❖ Founded in 1920 as New Haven YMCA Junior College, a division of Northeastern University.
❖ The institution became independent in 1926.
❖ In 1958 it was expanded, adding another building to keep up with the students coming in and the community. They added another three buildings and twenty-five acres in 1960 in West Haven.

Crew Afterthoughts

Raven: This was a very exciting investigation; seeing the orbs with the naked eye was awesome. I can't wait to go back.

Beckah: I want to go! I love the idea that not only Raven saw these bouncing orbs, but the other students as well! Now, if only we had the camcorder!

Katie: Connecticut is such a beautiful place to visit, even when one is not ghost hunting. I can't wait to get some time off—we are so going back. Oh yeah!

Mont Vernon Cemetery

*"A howling wilderness it was, where no
man dwelt. The hideous yells of wolves,
the shrieks of owls, the gobbling of turkeys,
and the barking of foxes were all the music we heard.
All a dreary waste and exposed to a thousand dif-
ficulties."*

—History of the Town of Mont Vernon,
New Hampshire, 1907

On a clear spring night, the Ghost Quest crew gathered together and decided we wanted to do something out of doors. The group hadn't hit a cemetery in a while and figured it was time to head back to our roots. Valley Street came to the forefront of our minds, and just when they were about to vote on it, the crew's guest, Julie, mentioned a place her and her husband went often looking for spirits called Mont Vernon. She mentioned that they often got voices there and mists; it could always be depended on for activity. They were greatly intrigued by her revelations and immediately hopped into our cars and headed toward the cemetery on a hill.

Twice over we got lost, due to our lack of attention, not spirit. After a couple of stops for coffee, we finally made it to our destination. Teren, another guest on our trip, and a gifted sensitive, immediately began to feel a protective presence within the gravesite. They split up into groups of two going off in their own directions, following our feelings and the energy. Julie went with Raven, Katie with Beckah, Fred with Doug and Teren.

Almost instantly, activity began. Every time Julie would take a picture of Raven, it was as though the spirits was assaulting her. There were hundreds of orbs clouding the picture, although when attempting to recreate the phenomena with another person, it could not be done. To Julie, it seemed the spirits had eyes only for Raven that night.

Doug, Fred, and Teren went on a search of their own. Traveling the perimeter of the cemetery, they took multiple shots that were littered with orb activity. They called out to spirits, asking for them to make their presence known. At that moment, something banged in the woods. The boys looked at each other and smiled. Unfortunately, there are some houses around the cemetery so we cannot confirm it was, in fact, spirit. But it was spooky.

Beckah and Katie went towards the left side of the cemetery. There the medium began to get pulled toward a medium-sized roughly-carved headstone. In front of it was a similarly rough-hewn bench, which Beckah straddled. She rubbed her hands over the headstone and felt a small vibration all through it. She knew someone was around her and began to make contact. "It's a man," she told Katie. "He is about thirty-two; he looks like he is from middle 1900s. I want to say thirties or forties; he calls himself Mark. He has brown hair and eyes, probably about five-six. What do you want to say hun?" She listens as the spirit communicates with her, "Yup, yup, okay hun; thank you for coming. He says he wants us to be careful here; there is a presence we need to watch out for."

Raven and Julie made their way to the far left corner of the cemetery. Immediately Raven had a reaction; she felt threatened. Fred, Doug, and Teren went to go see what was going on, as did Beckah and Katie. After we gathered and made sure Raven was okay, they began talking about what experiences they were having. Beckah related her story about the spirit named Mark and his warning, which also coincided with Teren's feeling of a protective presence.

As they walked together in the left-hand corner, Katie took pictures; the threatening presence continued to stalk us. As they rounded back toward the gate, the presence began to lessen, and as they walked through the gate, it left all together. They crew drove home, chattering excitedly. When Katie looked over the pictures of that night, her eyes lit up as she realized that's when Raven was having her attack, she'd caught a large red mist that took up half her photo. In the following photo, the red mist was more concentrated, both a darker red and a smaller amount, showing us that the spirit was really beginning to manifest. Besides that, there were orbs in quite a few pictures. Altogether, the group was excited about Katie's photos and couldn't wait to get back to head quarters and see the rest of our evidence.

When they got back, Rayna was ready with coffee and they were brewing with excited expectations. They looked over everyone's pictures, and while there were many with orbs, none were like the red mists Katie had captured. They got a few EVPs too. It was all in all a really fun and creepy case.

Evidence

There was very little hard evidence during this case. Below is a listing of evidence.

Photos:
Two pictures of red mist
Orbs surrounding Raven
Orb by Beckah during connection with Mark

EVPs:
"Look at Teren!" by a high-pitched female voice...very quick
"I don't know" in a male voice

Personal Experiences:
Doug felt as though he were being watched, the whole crew got the threatening feeling.

History of Mont Vernon
Cemeteries are just one small part of a community, and we must take a look at all the pieces of the puzzle to recognize the characters that may haunt the area.

❖ Mont Vernon was first settled in 1735 by Samuel Lamson and Samuel Walton both from Reading, Massachusetts.
❖ It was originally a part of Amherst; then it was char-

tered by a few other townships, until it officially became its own town in 1803.

❖ In the 1800s, Mont Vernon was known for its summer hotels. At this time, the population was under 800 people.

❖ The Mont Vernon Cemetery was established in 1781, and still has headstones from that time, including a unique headstone with a carved dog laying on it. To this day, the population remains just above 2,000.

Crew Afterthoughts

Raven: Wicked creepy cemetery at night; there are absolutely no lights. I kept seeing shadows of people walking out of the corner of my eye, sometimes standing next to crew members. It was SUPER CREEPY! Hearing the creature-like voice say our guest's name was weird. I want to go back…with big flashlights.

Beckah: Very interesting; I would like to go back and try to find out some history about the protective spirit. Connecting with Mark, although a short experience, was cool.

Katie: I can't believe I got a red mist that was so awesome! I would definitely like to go back there.

Manchester Enigma

"He won't scare you."

—EVP

A manager of a prestigious Manchester nightclub contacted us. It seemed some of the people who worked there, including the manager, had some close encounters of the ghostly kind while there late at night. Most of the occurrences were in the basement of the establishment, although they did report activity in by the bar as well.

Ghost Quest was excited about the call. After investigating many cemeteries, homes, and abandoned buildings, it would be refreshing to investigate a place that was occupied and active. Two of the crew went on a preliminary investigation. As they entered, Raven began to feel the familiar sensations that alerted her to the presence of spirits. She and Nancy met the manager at the door.

After talking to him, they descended down into the basement with cameras, camcorders, and tape players. The basement was well lit, clean, and somewhat orderly. As soon as the crew stepped off the staircase, Raven tapped into a male spirit. He seemed to have worked here when it was a butcher shop and the downstairs area was used for cutting and storing the meat. He told the medium his name was Marshall. It seemed he was happy to have finally found someone who could hear him and jabbered away about how life used to be for him. He talked about how when he worked here, it was a butcher shop and he managed downstairs which handled receiving shipments, cutting the meat, and storing it. He even told Raven where the freezer was located. He did admit to being a bit peeved with the current employees. They were too loud for him and there was always too much going on. He could never get his own work done.

He talked about his apprentice, Eddie, who was a lot like a son to him. "Eddie is grown up now," Marshall explained, "but he'll always be my boy." During his reminiscence, he discussed his family; he had two boys and a wife. They are with him now.

It seemed as Raven was relaying his every word to the rest of the crew, that Marshall seemed to snap out of the past and back into the present, seeing this as the opportunity to list all of his complaints. He said, "What I expect is cleanliness. They store their boxes all haphazardly in my area; I can't get work done like that!" He also complained about the owner stating, "He's got a stick up his a--." All of the above was confirmed by the manager, especially the last, which he laughed over.

When Raven asked why he was chuckling, he told her that they had just had a meeting in which a suggestion box was passed around. In it there was a slip with the words: Marvin has a stick up his a--! Raven rolled her eyes and laughed, as did Nancy.

Marshall was very active in the basement. Moving things around, turning on lights, touching or tapping people on the shoulder, things being thrown, and even faint whispering could be heard. None of this was done out of maliciousness. It was a need for people to stop and take a look at what they're doing. He loved his work. He didn't want to leave. With an understanding reached between Marshall the butcher and John the manager, we continued our investigation of the basement, although our new ghostly friend was still very territorial and decided to follow us, just in case we decided to move something else of his.

In the back room of the basement, as they talked, Raven heard the bang of something being thrown. It sounded like a rock or small object, but nothing was found. Although there was nothing of significance for the remainder of this part of the investigation, the group decided to come back as soon as possible with the whole crew.

No more than two weeks later, the crew stood in the main floor of the nightclub. Beckah looked around in wonder at the beauty of the room—birch branches covered the ceiling giving a rustic sophistication to the bar. But admiring the scenery was not what we were there for; our goal was to find out who was bothering the employees and the patrons of this fine establishment.

John told them that things down in the basement had calmed down, so they decided to tackle the upstairs. They set up our equipment with the idea of holding a couple of vigils where they would call out to the spirits asking for banging or movement of objects. We would also try glass divination to make contact with spirits. They knew there was definitely someone on this level and the crew wanted to really see what he or she could do. As Deana and Kelly walked the perimeter of the first floor gathering EVPs and photo evidence, Beckah and Raven set up the first vigil which would be glass divination.

They decided to do this first vigil as a group because they hoped to gather all the spirits to them, and figured they wouldn't freak as badly if everyone was there. It seemed as though no one wanted to speak, although they knew the spirits were there. Finally, after about five minutes, the group started to tap into a couple of the spirits, one of which was our dear friend, Marshall. They attempted to get the entities to move things or knock and rap. Glass sessions are much like Ouija boards. You ask questions and they answer, which they did, sparingly. The crew was a little disenchanted.

They decided to move the session to one of the bar tables in the back since that seemed to be where most of the spirit activity was. Raven tapped into a very large man who was manifesting at night before the club opened. He would move chairs, knock glasses over, and make ashtrays fly across the floor. Altogether not a fun guy, his name was William and he was passing through and "liked the place." He had no intention to leave. Since this was not a clearing session, the crew had no problem with him staying. He became very active on the board and it was a great session. After that, they decided to call again to see if they could get the spirits to knock and rap. Beckah did her best to get the spirits riled looking for any form of manifestation. She called, "C'mon you cowards, show me what you've got!" After twenty minutes of trying, Raven said: "Beckah knows you're here. I know you're here. But these three don't. Can you make a sound to prove that you're here?"

No one made a peep. As we all gathered together, thoroughly disheartened by the lack of audible phenomena, they drove home in silence, and started reviewing EVPs the same way. When they reached the end of the tape and Raven made the last ditch effort to get the spirits to make contact, a loud bang erupted from the other side of bar. No reaction was recorded, no one heard. But evidently the spirits were listening that night.

Evidence

At the Manchester Enigma site, evidence came to us in the forms of EVPs, pictures, and videos.

Photos:
> Main room orbs
> Basement energy
> Man watching from behind a pole
> Hand pointing down over bar
> Gentlemen in the mirror

EVPs:
> Marshall whistling (five instances)
> "Go"
> "He won't scare you"
> "Hi"
> Bang

Personal Experiences:
> There were no other personal experiences.

Crew Afterthoughts

Raven: Enigma was a kick, and getting in touch with Marshal was a real hoot! We knew that spirits often manifested sounds and voices on tapes alone because it takes lot less energy. However, hearing that big bang on the video and knowing we never actually heard it was cool and creepy.

Beckah: Very fun case! I loved the spirit board session and I think that the loud bang we heard was awesome. I am happy I got to meet Marshall who is an interesting character. William did scare me a little bit at first, and I think that although it wasn't a clearing session, I won't be surprised if we get called back to make him leave.

Katie: It sounded like it was an awesome experience! I hope we can do another case there so I can go.

Personal Experiences

"You can't move forward till you've looked at the past."

—Beckah

Although these are not technically Ghost Quest cases, they are odd stories from your authors' pasts, and give you a little bit more of an idea of how we got into ghost hunting in the first place.

Katie

I grew up in a small town called Goffstown, a town with a lot of old history. There, way up on a hill, was my big white house. From the age of two all the way up to seventeen, I lived there. When I was around five years old, my brother and I were playing in his room. He had two single beds and we were sitting on the floor with our backs resting on the side of his bed. My brother, as usual, was teasing me, not giving back my hot wheel cars. For some reason, I had turned my head and looked across the room at the door way. In plain view, a tall, burnt man stood almost reaching the top. He was covered in ash, with no body features showing. Blinded in fear, I remember screaming and running into the hall and bumped right into my mother. (She was skeptical about my experience, although she believed my fear.)

I experienced many strange occurrences from that day on. Every time I was alone in the house, a voice that sounded just like my father, would call out my name. Like I had said, I was always alone.

Feelings of being watched all through my house was an often occurrence. Every night until the age of about twelve, I would pull my bed covers over my head and fall asleep. At the age of eight, I started to become obsessed with the unknown. Sneaking down the road and visiting the local library, I would spend hours reading on paranormal topics and the occult. At one point, the librarian asked why I wanted to check out these kinds of books. My answer was always the same. "I'm doing a book report on this subject." I would smuggle most of those books home and hide behind the couch in the living room and read.

Every night around the same time, 12:00 am, I would have a nightmare and run into my parents' room. Ghostly images would fall upon my parents' bedroom walls, and I would stay awake until my eyes would force themselves shut. Some people would say, my nightmares were from all the books I was reading. I will have to disagree; for sometimes the images or shadows would talk and mumble. But also, my nightmares started *before* reading any books on the paranormal and occult.

Now our basement was a whole other story. Creepy, creepy, and for the love, don't make me go down there alone. Over one side of the basement was my father's work bench and his tools. The lighting was never very good, but something very negative was living in one of those dark corners. Built into one part of the wall was an old small vent-like door. Out of the corner of my eyes, I would catch a glimpse of a small creature climbing in and out of the door. The strange part was, the chamber was sealed. I could write a book in itself with all those experiences that happened in the house on the hill, but I'm getting creepy flashbacks of my childhood, so I'll stop here. If I only had a camera back then—darn!

Beckah

I loved our apartment in New Hampshire, it was an old gothic Victorian mansion turned into two-family apartments. My uncle owned it, and coming from Cambridge, I have to admit it was awesome having a yard. Our house was over two hundred years old, but in very, very good condition. There was a bedroom in the front of the house with a turret and all! It was so cool. That was my mother's room; then the parlor and another bedroom were side by side in the middle of the house. There was a large kitchen/dining room and bathroom, and last but not least, my room was all the way in the back. This was always the coldest room in the house, but being seventeen I was excited about the privacy. There was even my own exit, a set of old servant stairs leading down to the first floor. I only used them if I had to, though. I always felt there was someone there, chasing me when I had to use them, and I would run as fast as I could to get into my room.

Ever since I was little, I was a spiritual person, and when I hit eighteen, I had found direction. I began to work with spirits and to see them. But I still couldn't get over my fear of the man on the staircase. So my mother suggested I try having a conversation with him, so I did. I found out his name was Andreas, that he was from 1915, and he had been a servant during that time. I used to keep the door shut tight all the time. But as I became more comfortable with Andreas, I let it stay open, and as I fell asleep at night, I would look out onto the staircase and see him watching me.

Not many people would be able to sleep with a dead man watching them, but after I got to know him, he became a protective presence. One day, I was taking a picture of the mirror in my bedroom which I had handpainted, and in it, taking up all of the mirror was Andreas' face—so clear you could see the pores in his skin and his stringy black hair. I showed the picture to my mother and she got excited as well. I then talked to my aunt about what I saw and she agreed she too had always been tweaked by the stairs. From then on Andreas and I were as close to friends as spirit and a living person could be.

Another story about my room: My aunt's family originally owned the house and her grandfather, Jerry, lived in the back room I slept in. He also died in that room. I would smell pipe smoke, hear his footsteps going from the bed to the closet, and so on. My little sister actually made contact with him one night when she was about four years old. She woke up and told my mother she had dreamt of our grandfather, although when she described the man in her dream, it was in fact my aunt's grandfather, Jerry. He'd died before we moved up to New Hampshire and I never had the privilege of meeting him. He was a very active spirit within our apartment and we loved him. As I was opening up to spirits, things in my room got way more active, including him. I would hear him whispering as he paced, like he was thinking hard about something.

Anyway, it started when I was eighteen—the same time I came to terms with Andreas. I guess it was a big time for psychic activity because I was really opening to it. I always had problems sleeping; I wasn't an insomniac, but I had nights when I would have to fight to get some sleep. On one such occasion, it was a Wednesday night and it was around eleven thirty or so, I heard a man grunt and then what sounded like him falling to his knees and then flat to the ground. I looked out my window to make sure everything was all right, and it was, so I continued on my merry little way into dreamland. The next week it happened again, I knew then that it was spirit, but didn't know who. Was it from someone new?

I decided to ask my mother if she knew of any spirits who died of a heart attack, because that was what I felt with him. (By the way, even as I am writing this with Katie and Raven, I get the sensations of his death and smell his pipe smoke.) She revealed to me that Jerry himself had died of a heart attack. When I told her where in the room I was hearing it come from (near the right far corner), she confirmed it was the spot where he had passed away. This experience solidified my path, and cemented my beliefs in mediumship.

Raven

Although I have seen ghosts on and off throughout my life, the spirits from my early years always seemed to be kind and helpful spirits. It wasn't until much later that I began to connect with those who needed help or who were negative. Here are a couple of stories that really sent me on my journey into ghost hunting.

The first takes place in 1978 in the halls of Rindge and Latin High School. I was a sophomore on a mission. I had two very important reports to do and there was only one place I could think to do them—the library. Now, this library was a couple of hundred years old. The books dated back to the 1700s. I loved going in there and reading about, well, anything. Okay, I was a geek.

I will never forget it, as I crossed the courtyard to the library, I felt like I was being watched. I looked up to the third floor window and saw a woman staring down at me. She had sad eyes, Victorian clothing—I could see as far as her knees—and what appeared to be a noose around her neck. I quickly looked down at my books so that I didn't have to look at her.

As I entered the library I greeted the librarian who was quietly sorting through books and proceeded up to the second floor. I soon settled at a table to get to my work. The first peculiar thing I noticed was that there were no kids there. I knew people had classes, but usually at this time of day, you could hear all kinds of murmuring. Not on this day. It was silent. I shrugged my shoulders and got back to my work. After about twenty minutes of writing, yes this was before computers, I stretched my arms and as I looked up...there was the lady. She was there in full Technicolor looking back at me. I froze. She smiled and I could hear her in my head humming. She turned away and slowly faded into a back wall.

Later on, I asked some of the kids if they had ever seen the lady, and though none had, one of my friend's brother had. I regret that I didn't have the presence of mind to get the history of the lady with the noose. I may just have to do that.

The next story took place when I was eighteen and I was working at a nursing home in Cambridge. I was working on the eleven to seven shift, and lucky me, I had the second floor all to my self. This was the first time I'd worked upstairs and I had never heard anyone say anything about ghosts! Anyway, I was looking forward to getting caught up on my reading and was doing a good job of it. I checked my watch and did my rounds.

Afterward, I settled in for some more good reading. About a half hour later, I glanced up and one of the elderly ladies from the last room on the left was coming out of her room and walking towards me. As I watched her, she straightened up and was moving steadily holding on to her walker. I got up to meet her and guide her back to her room; and when I was three feet from her, she faded away. As unsettling as that was, it wasn't as unsettling as my next encounter there.

A bit stunned from what I had just experienced, I sat back down at the desk. I wiped the disbelief from my eyes and looked back down the hall. My mouth dropped and I sat staring. What I saw was a balding man's face and his rotund belly sticking out of the wall. He just stood there facing forward. As if this wasn't bad enough, at just that moment came a long wailing yell in a man's voice. I picked up my things, went downstairs, and demanded that if I was going to work upstairs, then someone was going to be with me. The head nurse told me to march back upstairs. I told her *I quit* and I did.

Appendix A
Spirits and Demons

Is Your House or Business Haunted?

Is Your House Haunted? Many people wonder whether or not their houses are haunted. Sometimes renovations can make a spirit act up—mostly because you're messing with their home. It will die down after the renovations are over. But for those that are not caused by redoing a home or building, there are different degrees of hauntings. See if your house fits any of the categories...

Mild Haunting

A mild haunting can consist of, but is not limited to: things going missing and turning up in the oddest places, smells that are often pleasant and invoke memories of times past (such as cigar, or flowers, or coffee brewing, or even perfumes), seeing things zip past you out of the corner of your eye, or seeing light shadows.

Also, you can experience hearing snippets of voice projections, like someone calling your name when no one is there. One other bit of phenomena is electronic equipment being turned on or off and phone calls with weird numbers or actual dates. Most of these spirits are family and friends who have crossed. Sometimes they are people who just wandered in or are in visitation because of a link with an item or place. If you wish to rid yourself of these spirits, usually all you need do is ask and they will leave, or they won't let you know they're about.

Moderate Haunting

A moderate haunting can consist of, but is not limited to: All of the above, but usually stronger or these things happen more often and to more than one person. Items may be removed completely, and sometimes, someone may be the target of such phenomena. Smells and voices can be stronger as well. These last longer in duration and usually become more active as time goes on. Hauntings of this type are usually from a spirit or spirits who are connected to the house, building, or land. It can also occur in cases where a spirit is trying to get an important message through. This type of haunting can be a bit jarring, but usually isn't harmful. If you wish for this type of spirit to leave, it can be done on your own, try asking first. If that doesn't work, it is better to have someone experienced do it for or with you.

Severe Haunting

This type haunting includes all of the above with differences. Smells can range from slight to quite foul. Objects can be thrown, people can be harmed (but not usually), loud noises can be heard, and things can disappear altogether. This type of haunting is usually with a spirit who is anchored to a place or land and is angry—maybe because of a violent death or other circumstances that were too horrific to him or her to get over. These spirits act out. The way to get rid of them is to have someone experienced clear them.

Demonic Haunting

This type of haunting is the scariest and most potentially harmful of all. Demons don't just come to a place or person; they are usually invited in, or they find a doorway. Phenomena is loud, abusive, and harmful. There can be noticeable fighting among those who live or work in the place, foul, horrible smells, and things or people being thrown or harmed. If it's not the place that is the center of activity, it can be a person that it is localized around. This is not a type of haunting to play around with. Leave the house or building. A demonologist or a cleric can clear them. Sometimes it is better to have both.

Ouija Session

A Word on Ouija Boards

There is a lot to be said on the use of Ouija boards. First lets set the record straight. OUIJA BOARDS ARE NOT EVIL!

Okay! Having said that, they are a portal. You can liken the use of a Ouija board with that of driving a car. If you don't know how to steer, don't get in the drivers seat! Ouija boards are a powerful tool to connect with spirits and other entities. You must remember that when you try to contact a spirit, you are literally asking for anything to come through, and most often times, that anything turns out to be negative. Why?

Because it is an easy way in. No trouble, no hassle, the humans are asking for it! There are ways of self protection that you can use when using a Ouija board.

Protect Yourself—Bubble Up!

What this means is to imagine God light above your table and see it pour down to envelop all those sitting there and yourself in a huge bubble. See it in your mind's eye as solid, love light. Nothing dark can penetrate it.

Ask For Help

Ask for higher spirits to come and guard your area to prevent negative spirits from coming in. These can be angels, guides, power animals, etc. Thank them when you're done.

Calling To Spirit

Lastly, ask for those beings who are there for your highest good to come and talk to you. Never put the call out to "anyone out there."

Either asking for help or calling for those who are for your highest good will keep you protected. But please, before you even think of pulling out the board, think about why you are using it. Do you want guidance, to help someone, to contact a loved one? Either way, be aware of the spirits you talk to, and be cautious about starting discussions with spirits you are not familiar with.

And last but not least always, ALWAYS Bubble up!

A Few Things to Watch Out For

Masking

Negative spirits, should they slip through, will sometimes mask as other people or loved ones. Ask a question that only you and the spirit you believe it to be would know. If the answer is incorrect end the session.

Heaviness

Your planchette will move at different rates as the spirits using it change. If it becomes very heavy or scraping on the board, end the session.

Outside Your Bubble Or Guarded Area

Phenomena can happen outside your bubbled or guarded area. Don't be afraid. If it begins to get a bit scary, end the session and send the bubble you erected out to cover the whole house. This should get rid of any minor negative that's around you.

Ouija Gibberish

Ouija Boards can be used safely. On rainy days it's one of our favorite ways to spend our meetings. We have also brought it with us to different locations, with spirit boards, it is always a hit or miss when it comes to clarity. Some spirits really know how to get their messages across, while others...well, they just don't know what they want to say. Here is a sample from one of our board sessions.

An Actual Ouija Session

Laughing of Raven and Beckah

Raven: If anyone's here for our highest good, please help guard us to keep out anything negative. So...

Beckah: No saying "whore." (This is in reference to a prior Ouija Board session.)

Raven: Is anyone here who would like to say hello to us?

Light planchette movement

Raven: *E, Q, D, R, I*

Beckah: Rayna get me a pen and a notebook!
Raven: What's this say?
Spirit: Hmmmm.
Raven: All right, is anyone pulling with the flow?
Beckah: What do you mean?
Raven: The planchett.
Beckah: No, I'm not thinking a damn thing and if I was thinking' something it wouldn't be *E-Q-D-I*.
Beckah: Eckter.
Spirit: E-quid.
Raven: E-quid. (In same tone as spirit)
Raven: What do you mean? What is *EQDIR*? What is it; can you clarify?
Raven: *S-I-M-P-J*
Raven: What does that mean? Simp J?
Spirit: No. (Same spirit)

Demonic Hauntings

Most of the hauntings we deal with are strictly spirit. A lot of the poltergeist activity is caused by a spirit who wants attention. But poltergeist phenomena on a larger scale can actually be a sign of demonic haunting. Spirits can cause small things to move or disappear such as your deodorant; a demonic would steal you mattress from the bedroom on the third floor and put it down in the basement. We are going to go over some more of the typical signs of a spirit haunting and compare them with a demonic house possession, we will also go over the steps of an inhuman entity would use to overtake a home and the people within it.

Spirits or Poltergeists
 ❖ Cause computers or electronics to act wonky, crash, or turn on and off
 ❖ Brings a thickness to the air
 ❖ Cause small arguments
 ❖ Create audible phenomena, knocks, footsteps
 ❖ Small items disappearing and reappearing, usually not very far from the spot taken

❖ Spirits can push or shove a person

Demonic or Inhuman Spirits
❖ Foul smells
❖ Furniture stacking
❖ Religious objects thrown or turned upside down
❖ Clicking sounds
❖ Small fecal balls being thrown through walls or dropped from ceiling
❖ Large items disappearing and reappearing in a different area in the house
❖ Physical harm can be experienced both internally and externally, bone breaking, bruising, in extreme cases death can occur.

Steps to a Demonic Possession
A demon's ultimate objective is to cause disruption and destruction. It will use whatever means to attain this goal, including house and bodily possession.

Invitation
Typically, this is done through a Ouija Board or other spirit communication device when used by those who have not been trained. Inhuman spirits can lay dormant within a home for years. Constant heated arguments, severe depression, debilitating addictions, or a person interested in the occult—these things will awaken a dormant demon.

Infestation
This is when they invite their friends in on the fun. They are not blatant about their activities, mainly staying in the humans' peripheral vision (usually little black balls of energy), and night time is usually much more active. They want to get you scared and keep you awake because this will cause you to eventually generate negative energy which will wear down the human will. Please consult a demonologist or paranormal investigator before assuming you have a demonic haunting.

Oppression

Divide and conquer; you are now engaged in war. The enemy can't be seen, but can be felt. They will bruise you, bite you, claw you, and screw with your mind, making you see your fears and become paranoid about the people around you, keeping you captive in your home. They will attack you day or night and show themselves usually to one person within the home. They manifest in whatever way they believe will scare you the most. Remember they are trying to keep you under their thumbs!

Possession

Your will is crushed and now they are in charge. Typically, they will only occupy the body for short amounts of time, leading to black-out periods. During this time they will destroy the people and things around you. They will continue to try and keep you isolated. Remember that there is always more than one, and even though you may not be possessed right now, that does not mean you aren't susceptible.

Appendix B
Ghost Hunting

Ghost Hunter's Glossary

Apparition
A full formation of a spirit.

Banishing
A ritual used to force an inhuman spirit to leave a home.

Cemetery
A plot of consecrated ground where the dead are buried.

Channeling
When a spirit enters a host body and uses it to communicate.

Channeler
Someone who has the ability to consciously allow or draw a spirit into their body and communicate with some degree of control, and the ability to make the spirit leave when the channeler feels the spirit is finished.

Cleansing
A ritual used to release negative energy from a home.

Clearing
A ritual used to force a spirit from a home.

Demonologist
A person who studies the hierarchy and lore of inhuman spirits, and typically studies with it occult sciences as well.

EMF
Electro Magnetic Field; it is believed that spirits are made up of this.

EMF Detector
Detects areas of concentrated Electro Magnetic Field.

EVP
An electronic voice phenomena; it is when an audio recorder catches a spirit talking or creating noise.

Grounded Spirit
This is a spirit who has not been to the "other side." This could be for a multitude of reasons. Often it is because they want their story told, because they were afraid to go; or sometimes, in quick deaths, it can be they just aren't aware of their current state of existence.

Haunted
Inhabited by or visited regularly by a ghost or other supernatural being.

Inhuman Spirits
Most of the spirits we talk about have lived and died. Inhuman means these spirits have never touched the Earth as a living organism.

Medium
People with the ability to get in contact with the dead.

Mists
Often created when spirits begin to fully form.

Occult Science
The study of ancient signs, symbols, and rituals related to magic.

Orb
It is the easiest way for spirits to travel as it doesn't take much energy. Often seen as balls of light, sometimes they can have tails when in motion.

Parapsychology
The study of energy, spirits, and unexplained phenomena.

Paranormal Phenomena
Events that are unable to be explained or understood in terms of scientific knowledge.

Poltergeist
A supposed supernatural spirit that reveals its presence by creating disturbances, for example by knocking over objects, levitating items, and turning on and off lights.

Psychic Sensitive
A person who can sense a change in energy around them, feels presences easily but may not be able to gather clear information about the spirits they sense are around them.

Spirit
The life force of a once-living individual or animal.

Visitation
Spirits come to places and people they love and remember after they have gone over to the "Other side" to see how things are going. They also tend to gather with living family and friends when there is distress around them.

Ghost Quest's Beginners Guide To Equipment

This is a guide based on what we at Ghost Quest used when we first began our ghost hunting. It worked for us and hopefully it will work for you!

EVP'S
What can you use to get great EVPs?

Any Sony tape recorder is awesome. They pick up literally everything around you, both physical and ghostly. We have gotten some of our best EVPs using our Sony tape recorder, and the best thing is it wasn't overly expensive.

Pictures
How can I take awesome pictures?

Any good digital camera will work. We use Olympus and Fuji Cameras. Both inexpensive as cameras go, but they take great photos. It just proves that you don't have to pay hundreds of dollars for a top notch camera.

If you have a tight budget, disposable digital cameras or thirty-five millimeter cameras will give you good results.

Videos
How can I take great videos?

Any good video camera will work. Sony and Panasonic are both great cameras. Make sure it has an IR filter or night vision integrated in it, and for ease of use, a good fire wire connection and movie development software will help.

Temperature Scanner
What type of temperature reader should I get?

For this, buy a top-notch device that has scanning capability. We use one put out by Radio Shack. This will help when you are moving the gauge around an area.

EMF Detector
What's an EMF Detector and should I have one?

We use an ElectroSensor. You can easily find this on the internet and it's not that expensive. It measures these frequencies in the air. It has been found that when these frequencies spike, there is likely to be a manifestation of spirit phenomena.

Appendix C

Resources

Resource List

Historical Resources

www.goffesfalls.org — Manchester Historical Site
www.data.visionappraisal.com/ManchesterNH/ — Property Data Manchester, NH
http://i-cias.com — For information on the Phoenician's God Ba'al
http://www.valley-cemetery.com — Friends of Valley Street Cemetery

Paranormal Websites

www.ghostquest.org — NH's Paranormal Research Society
www.ghosttown.com — Haunted locations
www.shadowland.com — Haunted locations
www.njghosts.com — New Jersey Ghosts
www.paranormalplace.com — Paranormal Place
www.warrens.net — Ed and Lorraine Warren
www.chosenones.net — The search for the chosen ones
www.utyx.com/paranormal/ — Paranormal
www.everythingparanormal.com — Everything Paranormal
www.2getgold.com/california/haunted/haunted_hollywood.html — Haunted Hollywood
www.ghost-story.co.uk — Ghost Stories UK
www.chasingmidnight.com — Chasing Midnight
www.ghosts-uk.net — Ghosts UK
www.essexparanormal.net — Essex Paranormal
www.hampshireghostclub.net — Hampshire Ghost Club
www.evp-voices.com — EVP Voices
www.worldofghosts.co.uk — World of Ghosts

www.epiphanyslight.com — Epiphanys Light
www.anzwers.org/free/ghosts beyond/ — Ghosts from Beyond
www.ghostvillage.com — Ghost Village
www.edenseve.net — Edens' Eve
www.ghostfiles.org — Ghost Files
www.wirenot.net — Archive X
www.home.austarnet.com — Under The Bridge
www.theloneconspirators.cjb.net — The Lone Conspirators
www.trueghoststories.co.uk — Real life ghost stories
www.trueghosttales.com — True Ghost Tales
www.hauntednations.venableswebdesigns.com — Haunted Nations

Paranormal Television Shows

CWT Network: *Supernatural*
The Biography Channel: *Dead Famous*
The Discovery Channel: *A Haunting*
The Discovery Channel: *Haunting Evidence*
Court TV: *Psychic Detectives*
SciFi Channel: *Ghost Hunters*
Travel Channel: *Most Haunted*

Paranormal Radio

Sightings with Jeff Rense
Mysteries of the Mind
Ground Zero with Clyde Lewis
Laura Lee Online
The ParaNet Continuum
The X-Zone
The Lou Gentile Show
Night Search
The Next Dimension
World of the Unexplained
A Glimpse Through The Veil
A.P.S.R. Paranormal Talk Radio
Ghostly Talk

Reality and Beyond
21st Century Radio
The Allan Handelman Show
The Kevin Smith Show
The Jerry Pippin Show
Wake Up USA
Jane Doherty
Strange Days
Higher Minds
Future Talk
Grand Deceptions